What Others are Saying About
The After Party of the Empty Nest

After our first left the nest last year, I kept telling anyone who would listen, "Why doesn't anyone warn you how hard this is?" FINALLY, a resource to both warn and support parents through the transition that can hit you like a Mack truck. I had no clue what I was walking into. I'm so grateful that Kate is now on the journey with me."

~**Lisa-Jo Baker,** bestselling author of
Never Unfriended and *It Wasn't Roaring, It Was Weeping*

Kate Battistelli has written the book every empty-nest mom needs. *The After Party of the Empty Nest* is a warm, hope-filled guide reminding us that life doesn't end when our children leave home—it expands in beautiful and unexpected ways. With wisdom, practical advice, and a dash of spunk, Kate encourages moms to embrace this season with faith, purpose, and joy. If you're feeling the ache of an empty house, let Kate's words uplift your heart and remind you that your best years are still ahead. This book is a must-read!

~**Tricia Goyer,** USA Today
Bestselling Author of 90+ Books,
including *Faith That Sticks* and *Heart Happy*

The After Party of the Empty Nest, by Kate Battistelli, is a much-needed conversation for moms who have often been neglected or told to move on once their children are grown and out of the home. And if there is ever a voice that *should* speak into it, it's Kate. Finally, we have someone who has turned the fear and struggle of this season into a great adventure with Jesus. If your children have left your home, or they're about to, prepare your heart to see the goodness of God in it by reading this book.

~**Brooke McGlothlin**, founder of Million Praying Moms and author of *Praying for Teen Boys: Partner with God for the Heart of Your Son.*

"In *The After Party of the Empty Nest,* Kate lovingly yet firmly takes moms by the hand and helps them not only navigate the empty nest years but dare to dream again. I love that each chapter contains questions for discussion, Scriptures, and a prayer—making it perfect for small groups. Kate's passion to encourage moms right where they are shines through this beautiful book from beginning to end."

~**Stacey Thacker,** Author of *Praying for Teen Girls*

In *The After Party of the Empty Nest,* Kate Battistelli prepares moms for the "catch and release" of motherhood and the realities of an empty nest. With heartfelt wisdom and practical advice, Kate provides the next stage of mentoring most women desperately need. All moms should read this book to be ready to feather a new nest when their babies spread their wings and start to fly.

~**Rachel Dodge,** author of *The Anne of Green Gables Devotional, The Little Women Devotional,* and *The Secret Garden Devotional*

I have watched Kate's empty nest journey in real time, unfolding into her beautiful after party. With truth and grace, Kate helps us all prepare for this inevitable transition. Kate's words are strung together with poise, one mother comforting another but giving us all the nudge to remember our purpose. Mothers desperately need this book, like a new song in the night. Great work, Kate!

~ **September McCarthy,** Empty Nester in
slow motion and Author of {Why} Motherhood
Matters and Hope for Your Homeschool, Start
Strong, Stay the Course, Finish with Joy

Every believer at EVERY stage in life is called to live out the purpose God has for us, whether as a teen, young parent, or empty nester. As a full-time mother of four, the wisdom I've received from others who've raised children to love and serve the Lord has helped me teach my four children to do the same. I'm grateful for Kate's new book. Each day has its challenges, but when empty nesters take the time to help full nesters, it encourages and gives breath to the weary, worn-out mother on a mission.

~**Tina Griffin,** TV/radio host of The
Counter Culture Mom Show

The After Party of the Empty Nest is the trusted guide every mom of young adults needs to prepare for launch day. She packs every page with the hard-won wisdom and biblical insight of a seasoned mother who has experienced an empty nest's pain, purpose, and even pleasure. In your next chapter, Kate Battistelli will help you redefine your role and reimagine what life can look like.

~**Jamie Erickson,** author of *Holy Hygge* and
co-host of The Mom to Mom Podcast

THE AFTER PARTY OF THE EMPTY NEST

THE AFTER PARTY OF
THE EMPTY NEST

Mom is Not Your Only Name

KATE BATTISTELLI

DEDICATION

To Mike Battistelli,
You are and always will be my puzzle part,
the best parenting partner,
husband above all others,
and a dad to beat all other dads … but God.

To Francesca Battistelli Goodwin,
You made me a mother
and you made me love mothering.
You helped me see my empty nest
as both an opportunity and a challenge
only you and your dad could walk me through.

TABLE OF CONTENTS

Note from the Author · xi
Introduction · xiii

The Truth · 1
Chapter 1: Moving from Mom to Empty Nest Mom · · · · · 3
Chapter 2: How Empty Nest Moms Face a
      Change of Seasons · 15
Chapter 3: Seasons Season Us · · · · · · · · · · · · · · · · · · 25
Chapter 4: Many Empty Nest Moms are Saying:
      "What Do I Do with All My Time?" · · · · · · · · · · · 35
Chapter 5: Many Empty Nest Moms Agree:
      The After Party is Good · · · · · · · · · · · · · · · · · · 45

The Challenge · 53
Chapter 6: Many Empty Nest Moms Say:
      The After Party is Hard · · · · · · · · · · · · · · · · · · 55
Chapter 7: Three Truths to Help You Cope with Your
      Empty Nest · 65
Chapter 8: For the Empty Nest Mama Whose
      Child has Walked Away from Their Faith:
      Praying for Prodigals · 73
Chapter 9: A Premature Empty Nest … and
      a Beautiful Trust · 83

The Work · 91

Chapter 10: Empty Nest Moms and the Power of Prayer · · ·93

Chapter 11: God Is in the Details · · · · · · · · · · · · · · · ·101

Chapter 12: The Empty Nest is the Perfect Season
    to Dream with the Father · · · · · · · · · · · · · · · ·111

Chapter 13: The Destiny of the Diligent:
    Seven Ways to Prepare Now for Then · · · · · · · · · ·125

Chapter 14: An Empty Nest and the Value in
    Volunteering ·133

The Focus ·139

Chapter 15: Marriage First...You Are More Than
    Roommates ·141

Chapter 16: Rediscovering Dating...Your Husband · · ·151

Chapter 17: Single Moms and the Empty Nest · · · · · · ·161

Chapter 18: Dear Empty Nest Mom:
    Self-Care is Not Selfish · · · · · · · · · · · · · · · · · ·171

Chapter 19: How Empty Nest Moms Can Bridge
    the Generation Gap: Mentoring Matters · · · · · · · ·183

The Future ·199

Chapter 20: Hindrances to Your After Party:
    Six Traps that Could Frustrate Your Future · · · · · · ·201

Chapter 21: If You Don't Know Where You're Going,
    How Will You Know When You Get There? · · · · · ·211

Chapter 22: Catch and Release · · · · · · · · · · · · · · ·217

Chapter 23: Let's Party! · · · · · · · · · · · · · · · · · · · 223

For Additional Reading · · · · · · · · · · · · · · · · · · · 229

Acknowledgments ·231

About the Author · 235

Other Books by Kate ·237

Songbirds are taught to sing in the dark.

Oswald Chambers, *My Utmost for His Highest*

NOTE FROM THE AUTHOR

There are two ways moms experience an empty nest: launching their last or only child into the world or watching as their older children begin to move out while they still have younger children at home. Their nests aren't completely empty, but they continue to shrink year by year as their children grow and go. Like the mom sending her last one out, she will likely deal with many of the same challenging and complex emotions every time another child leaves.

This book addresses both categories of moms. If your last child is heading out or has already left, you may find yourself completely unprepared, as I was when the shock of my empty nest hit me hard. Uncertainty, bewilderment, and a cloud of unknowing can cause anxiety and trepidation as we're forced to face this new reality.

For moms whose children are departing one by one, I have included what I trust will motivate and empower you to begin planning *now* for *then*, helping you avoid making the same mistakes I made.

I pray *The After Party of the Empty Nest* will bless and encourage you, reminding you that an After Party awaits offering you a new future and a fresh purpose.

INTRODUCTION

Mama, before we jump in, let me assure your heart with this: as hard and heart wrenching as this next stage might look to you right now, *you will survive.* I'm lovingly taking your face in my hands, looking into your eyes, and assuring you that you *can* get through the empty nest season. As daunting as it may seem today, life *will* return to a new version of normal. Ask every question racing through your heart. We will explore them together.

As your perspective shifts, you'll discover joy, purpose, and success as your life moves into a brand-new phase. You are heading into a fresh and rich adventure if you release the old and grab hold of the unfamiliar. Think of it like a treasure hunt–you never know what you might find!

In these pages, you will hear real stories from real women. Some are messy, some beautiful. Stories that are painful, hopeful, bruised, inspiring and more. You will meet them in day-to-day life and read their stories of redemption, marriage, parenting, singleness, loss, heartache, and the joy of a job well done.

The empty nest is not an end, but a sacred migration as God guides us to soar higher into a fresh adventure for our lives. – Kate

Hang in there with me as we explore this treasure hunt together.

Invitation to the Party

With trembling hands and the foreboding feeling that it isn't good news, a mom cautiously tears open an envelope. The invitation reads something like this:

Dear Mom,

**You are cordially invited to a party. *An After Party.*
Your children are growing up, and soon,
they will be heading out of the nest.
All those years of loving and sacrific-
ing, cooking and cleaning,
disciplining and discipling, bargaining and praising,
yelling and listening are all coming to
an abrupt and unceremonious end.
This is your formal invitation to the next act ... to
Motherhood: The After Party.
*Because Mom is NOT your only name.***

Date and Time: After your children leave the nest.
Place: Wherever dreams can go.
Dress Code: Come as you are.
RSVP: No need to reply ... attendance is mandatory.

Not all moms are alike. As I've studied this empty nest stage of life and the various ways we can handle it, I imagine the stages as three distinct types of mama birds. Like us, each mama bird must determine to carry on as her fledglings fly from their warm and comfy nests. The three birds I believe represent these stages the best?

- The Swallow.
- The Mourning Dove.
- The Robin.

The graceful **Swallow,** with her shimmering and iridescent feathers, is a social and happy little songbird. Because Swallows are migrating birds, they can adapt easily to new environments. As her chicks head out, the classic empty nest Swallow mama spreads her wings, as she eagerly explores new horizons. She is happy to have her life back, and though she will experience the same sense of loss all moms feel, she revels in her new-found freedom, excited to explore all life has to offer.

Swallow moms enjoy more time to spend with their husbands and the opportunity to pursue projects or dreams they put on the back burner while raising their children.

Mourning Doves, with their soft plumage and gentle coos, are tender and unassuming birds. They are powerful flyers and remarkable navigators, traditionally representing peace, love, and hope. But on the flip side, because of their soft melancholy cooing, we often associate them with mourning and loss.

The Mourning Dove mom grieves her empty nest as happy memories of the past churn up deep emotions. Her memories give some solace but can't fully soothe her heavy heart. It may take her a bit more time to overcome sorrow and adjust to her new role.

Robins, those heralds of spring, are a blend of both. With their colorful red breasts, they are friendly yet territorial birds. I'm intrigued that the Robin population is estimated to be 310 million and is America's third most common bird.

Robin empty nest moms are the most prevalent as well, as they quickly adapt to their next season while experiencing a mix of emotions. They miss the past but eagerly anticipate the future. They are typically quite resilient and well-equipped, quickly adjusting to this new stage of life. As they encounter change, after a time they find they can anticipate a completely new season.

Each of these three mamas will approach their empty nests differently, but as they persevere, they will discover a new and reassuring equilibrium. As complicated and taxing as it feels at first, all three mama birds eventually find a way through.

I encourage the empty nest moms I encounter to feel all the feels ... tears, laughter, sorrow or relief. Take a moment and thank the Lord for your years with your child. Your relationship doesn't end, but it does change. Even though it may feel like it some days, you haven't been downsized as a mother.

The only way out of grief and heartache
is to go through it. – Kate

What type of mama bird best describes you? As time goes on, it may very well change. But rest assured that eventually, all three will find a brand-new flight path in these new and uncharted skies.

When the Truth of My Empty Nest Hit Out of the Blue

The first morning my daughter—my only child—was gone, I woke up, grabbed my coffee, and—on auto-pilot—headed to the living room for our daily quiet time of spiritual reflection before the day took us in different directions. Except I was alone. She was gone. Sitting there in a puddle of tears, the loss weighed heavy on my heart as I realized my life had abruptly rearranged. The silence and finality of it all were deafening.

It felt perfectly natural to send our daughter off to meet her future. But I'd had no idea how quickly the past would rear its ugly head, reminding me my active parenting season—what I'd poured myself into for two decades—was over.

No more quiet times together in the morning, no spontaneous shopping trips to the mall, no lively lunches and dinners out. No more family movies on the couch or the easy camaraderie we had always known. The walls and floors of my house echoed with the memories of meals shared, tantrums tamed, giggles, hugs, and tears, crying at Hallmark movies, tickle fights on the sofa, and so much more.

And as the mom of an only child, there were no "backup siblings" to help lessen my loss.

It was how it was supposed to be, but who was *I* supposed to be? I was still a mom, yes, but my role had morphed into something foreign. I faced a complete surrender to that gray zone between the loss of my purpose and the gain of new possibilities.

As time passed, I discovered a new direction, a new calling, and a new and utterly unexpected future. It came in fits and starts. But eventually I found my way to a purpose I never expected and certainly never planned for. But it took some time.

> *Every day holds a future we've yet to meet. This is the day the Lord has made… even the hardest ones. – Kate*

I realized I was the classic Robin mom, looking forward to what might come next, yet not ready to give up control as I longingly looked back at what I'd had. I knew I was facing a new and very uncertain future. Forced to fast forward, all I wanted to do was rewind. As proud as I was to watch my daughter plunge headlong into her calling, at the same time, I had to let go of my identity as the main human in her life, the one she looked to for advice, encouragement, and approval.

My husband and I had done all we could to prepare her for adulthood. We gave her the map to follow—with all the warnings, love, and support possible—and sent her on her way. But how do you let go of what you've always known? How do you embrace a new and unfamiliar future?

Let me assure you it is worth every tear, every prayer, and every moment of worry or fear for the days ahead. There is no shame in grieving what you are leaving behind and no shame in searching for answers.

> *Reality can bruise us if we don't accept it. – Kate*

Motherhood is both a beautiful dance and a brutally gut-wrenching exercise in self-control. As much as we want to jump in and solve every one of our children's problems, we must now sit on the sidelines, letting them learn to live without us. And as *they* begin to learn, *we* learn something too. We learn to pray without ceasing. And we learn God has an Act II just for us.

Raising children to be capable adults is one of the most amazing, agonizing, beautiful, and painful things we will ever do. We celebrate our children's independence while mourning their departure. In fact, if we grieve their going, we most likely did it right.

I had no idea of the surprises God had in store for me, and He has them for you, too. Yes, your children are heading out, and yes, it hurts. But if you hand your future to God, you will find He has more up His sleeve for you than you can imagine.

When I speak to women's groups about the empty nest, these are the standard questions they ask me:

- Who am I now?
- What is my purpose now that my children are gone?
- What gifts and talents do I have to offer?
- What is important?
- What should my priorities be?
- What is my parenting role now?
- How do I become something more than "Mom?"

Having the house to yourself and the opportunity to come and go as you please is nice, but for many moms it is a far cry from having your kids there every day. We have been their cheerleaders for nearly two decades, but who is cheering *us* on?

It's fine to ask all these big questions, especially when we feel overwhelmed. We are *forced* to embrace change. We aren't asked if we want to feel unexpected and conflicting emotions. Now, we have no choice but to navigate a landscape as unfamiliar as an undiscovered island.

There is no other option. We *must* learn to navigate that brand-new landscape. Yet at the same time, fresh opportunities beckon. The future is just over the horizon with adventures we've never even thought to ask for. It may be hard to believe right now, but your empty nest is actually a good problem!

When our children were little, it was simple to put off thinking about the empty nest.

As Scarlett O'Hara expressed at the end of "Gone with the Wind": *"I can't think about that right now. If I do, I'll go crazy. I'll think about it tomorrow."*

So, we ignore it until it sneaks up and smacks us in the face with the truth of its inescapable finality. Without much warning, a new reality hits like a gut punch. We are no longer the loudest voice in their heads, and they are no longer our primary identity or responsibility.

It's a delicate balancing act. We live in the *now* while preparing for *then*–that uneasy season when our last child leaves their safe and comfortable nest, venturing out into the big, wide world *without us*. It can be daunting and difficult to wrap our minds around.

This is the reality. You are now mom to a grown child or children, officially a parent of an adult or adults. You are not him or her, and your personality is likely quite different.

Unlike my daughter, I'm a fixer, a problem solver, and solution oriented.

Whenever my daughter came to me with a heartache or challenge, my immediate response was to hold onto control and do what I could to solve it. It's the way I'm wired. But sometimes, she didn't want a solution. Sometimes, she only needed me to listen and give her a hug and tell her I loved her.

As a Robin mom, I had to face the fact that I was holding on too tight. Sometimes I *couldn't* fix it, which was okay because she didn't need it to be fixed. I had to learn to let go and help her figure it out for herself. How would she learn if I kept solving every trial she faced? She needed only one thing: someone to listen.

Some Swallow moms may be more laid back or *laissez faire* in their approach to their child's issues or concerns. They've been here before with them and can view their issues as an opportunity compelling their child to grow. They know they will figure it out on their own.

Melancholy or Mourning Dove moms might commiserate with their child, feeling all the emotions while at the same time, able to offer both understanding and advice.

Our children *will* grow up, and as they do, their gaze turns upward and outward. They are living out our legacy but must learn to untangle and unravel life's adventures for themselves. Our job is to remember *we are not them*, and we can no longer make everything right, solve every problem, and remove every obstacle. We must continue to live our own lives, not theirs.

I think this particularly applies if you are the parent of an only child.

We can become so wrapped up in our children's lives that we forget to focus on our own. And for some of us, realizing we are facing an empty nest this year or in the next few years sets off alarm bells in our hearts. It dawns on us that one day, our children will go. *Motherhood is a journey of letting go.* And that's the hardest but most necessary part... to *let* them go.

> *In the quiet of an empty nest, God invites us*
> *to release our children with faith, trusting*
> *fully in His sovereign plan.* – Kate

It helps to thoughtfully look ahead now and consider what we will face while we still have kids at home.

Our lives are busy. It's natural to brush aside thinking about the inevitable day when our children *will* leave home. But when we do, we find ourselves facing a serious sea change as we gradually realize that every day, our children simply need us a little less.

We peek into the future, our view dim and cloudy, seeing no clear path ahead. We have been so immersed in their lives that we have neglected to plan for our own. We might feel consigned to the margins, left outside and on the edge of everything we've known.

It is easy to define ourselves by what we do or who others say we are. But as women of God, we are not defined by the roles we play, even as those roles were the joy of our lives. We are who God created us to be–not a role but a person whose identity is defined and whole in Christ. He gives us the help we need and prepares us for the other half of our life... *a life without kids.*

Stick with me, mama. You are not past your prime. God has so much more!

When my After Party invitation arrived, it hit me like a ton of bricks. Hot tears stung my eyes, and truth crushed my heart as the hard fact of it all sunk in. *What's my identity now?* Sitting in my overly silent and nearly vacant house, these words raced through my brain: *"So, this is what an empty nest looks like. Emptiness."*

Reality sank in, and only this thought took root in my aching heart.

"Am I done being a mom?"

Questions raced and confusion churned. "Is this it? Seriously? They pack up and go, and that's supposed to be okay? What am I supposed to do *now*? I've poured out every ounce of myself for years on end, and this is what I get? A silent house? No one needing me? No purpose, no point....*no noise?*"

As the Mourning Dove mom in me took over, I felt my heart had been shattered against a brick wall. Why? Because I had not planned for it. I had hardly *thought* about it. My days of active mothering were over, but I'd never taken the time to look ahead and plan. All my energies stayed focused on the pressing needs of "now."

My nest was empty...and so was my heart...and my house.

But let's be honest. How on earth can you plan for your future when mothering takes every ounce of everything you've got? Our lives overflow with countless chores devouring our time day in and week out. Most of us find it overwhelming, especially if we have more than one child. Even those of us with an only child deal with the often monotonous and seemingly endless daily tasks.

I know how hard you work. You cook and clean, do laundry and carpool, budget wisely, discipline, organize schedules, run errands, attend school events, and on and on it goes. I bet you could add many more tasks to the list. Maybe you even work full or part-time.

Mothering is a delicate, daily balancing act. With all the joy raising children brings, moms grapple with endless activities, unrelenting, unceasing, and overwhelming at times. We make every effort to find a proper balance between our responsibilities and remembering to take care of ourselves. We are determined to do all we can to stay as healthy and strong as possible to accomplish the work we must do each day while raising our family.

But we put so much energy into caring for others that it is easy to forget about ourselves. A crying baby or a sick toddler can easily eclipse prayer time, Bible study, or a workout at the gym. Stopping at the drive-thru is much faster and less stressful than making a nourishing meal at home. I get it. Some days, you've got four kids in the car, the two-year-old is having a meltdown, everyone is starving, and the thought of making lunch for a crew is overwhelming ... and like a siren song, Chik-fil-A beckons ... with a side of guilt.

It's hard enough planning nutritious meals for the week or activities for summer break, preparing your weekly homeschool lessons, or driving your kids to practice to even *think* about a time when your children won't be around to plan for anymore. It's arduous in the trenches and hard to imagine a time when they'll be grown. And gone.

It makes sense that the day we retire is not the day to start planning financially for retirement. It's way too late then. But when it comes to the empty nest phase of life, isn't that too often how we handle it? It creeps up on us before we've given a thought to getting ready for it.

I guess I should have thought about it more, but how do you fully prepare for this kind of life change? It's a heady cocktail of contradictions, and like a massive waterfall, it rushes headlong, overwhelming you completely. (Like menopause or childbirth. Am I right?)

THE TRUTH

CHAPTER 1

Moving from Mom to Empty Nest Mom

M ost moms know that the most arduous stage of labor is *transition*. A tidal wave of unrelenting contractions takes over our bodies, one piling on top of another. Our only thought is, *how do I get off this train and go home?* It's the toughest part of the process. Those helping with your birth cheerily remind you that your baby is right around the corner. Some of us want to punch them for that ill-timed advice! It doesn't help, especially when you feel like a humongous watermelon is about to break through your swollen belly after what can amount to *hours* of pain and pushing.

Birth is a battle. Most of us have pushed our babies into our world. Now is the moment to push them into *their* world and future.

My husband and I used to be certified instructors in the Bradley Method of Natural Childbirth, designed for women who want an unmedicated birth with minimal intervention. We were blessed to coach many laboring women. When we lived in New York City, it would not be unusual for my husband, Mike, to come home to our small condo after conducting a show uptown to find a laboring woman and her somewhat perplexed husband being coached through early labor.

As labor progressed, I would work to adjust Mom's focus off her pain and onto the prize, reminding her that as difficult and painful as it seemed at that moment, *she could do this.* She was perfectly designed to do this. She and her husband had waited nine long months, and if they could press into the pain a little longer, their precious baby would soon be in their arms.

The transition stage affected each labor differently. I noticed it tended to last the longest for the moms who fought against it rather than the ones who relaxed (as much as possible) and allowed labor to run its natural course.

Honestly, it is not much different than sending your children out into the big, bad world. We can wring our hands, gnash our teeth, and emotionally stress at the thought of their leaving home, or we can relax and cheer them on, trusting we have done our job as we rest in knowing that God has their lives and futures firmly in hand.

We have raised our children in the knowledge of Christ, but we can never force them to follow. God creates their character, we model it, but the Holy Spirit molds it in them. We would be delighted to see it fully shaped when they are grown and out of the house, but His ways and timelines are not ours. Don't give up!

Gina

The ache did not leave right away. When they moved out, it felt like my purpose and my heart had moved out with them.

Of course, there would be some grieving! How could I NOT grieve? They are my most precious gifts from God! It has taken time to figure out and adjust to what life looks like now, but I have adjusted.

Bringing home a newborn was one of the hardest seasons I have experienced. I was crazy about my babies, but learning a new way of living was hard. I eventually found a new rhythm and got used to caring for a baby and getting little sleep! Sending my children out 20+ years later was just as hard, if not harder, than when I brought them home. Both seasons were huge and life-altering.

There is a promise I have been clinging to in a new way as we have entered the empty nest season – the promise that God will provide grace for each moment.

⚖

As we raise our children, each season seems to organically transition into the next. A few of those transitions are seamless and painless. Some are abrupt and, without warning, sideswipe us out of nowhere … like the terrible twos or the sudden onset of teenage hormones. Others require digging deep and trusting God with everything we have. But Jesus reminds us that He will guide us through each and every season. Our job? Do our best to relax and *be anxious for nothing* (Philippians 4:6), knowing He will give us exactly what we need *exactly* when we need it.

But I am not gonna lie, mama. It's hard. Aside from having our first baby and learning all we need to know to care for and raise an infant, an empty nest is one of the biggest transitions we will ever experience. All we have known and worked hard to nurture and maintain morphs into a new reality *in a day*. Suddenly, every part of every single day feels upended.

That day becomes both a promise for the future and a stinging reminder of the past. The old and new rhythms collide, reminding us that our life is no longer what it was. But now, as we toggle between what was and what will be, who will *we* be? When our children leave the nest, they must discover who they *actually are*, not who we have said they are.

> *As our children move into their independent*
> *lives, in time, we will come to realize that their*
> *departure isn't desertion, but a proud affirmation*
> *of a parenting role well done.* – Kate

As we send them off to college or the airport or their own apartment or job, the worst bit is letting go of that final fervent hug, dispensing that parting piece of sage advice. We hold back tears as we wave good-bye, straining to rubberneck from the sidelines as they plunge headlong into their new lives. You might be releasing your only child or your oldest child. The pain is the same, no matter their chronological order. Pain needing to be respected and understood.

It's normal to grieve this change. We are thrust into the undiscovered world of God's plans for us. After my daughter left home, regardless of my emotions and opinions about it, I knew my purpose and the entire focus of my life had shifted. As much as I wanted to hold onto my control with clenched fists, I had to face one fact: that season was done forever…and though the loss gnawed deep in my soul, it was thrilling to see her march fearlessly into her calling.

Staring squarely at my empty nest forced me to realize my role as Mom hadn't come to an end. It was simply one of every mom's necessary transitions. My position may have shifted, but I was still, and always would be, Mom.

When our children make their first visit home over the holiday break, we find ourselves back in our favorite happy mom-place once more. As break ends, they leave us to go back to school or their job, and we must let them go *all over again*. The tough truth is this: they simply do not need us the way they used to.

For most moms, the hardship of the empty nest is short-lived. Many of us typically begin to enjoy life again in a few months as our Robin mom takes over. However, moms of onlys (like me), single moms, moms of children who have joined the military, and moms in unhappy marriages are more susceptible to a longer period of emotional upheaval.[1]

The Lonely Middle

At the start of the empty nest, we find ourselves swimming in that lonely and messy middle, the time between seasons when we feel the ache of losing the past but are beginning to awaken to a brand-new purpose as the future beckons.

Because our children have been much of the focus of our lives for so long, we may endure a time of heartache as we begin training for a wholly new chapter. We might feel dread, depression, and sadness when they leave. An empty hole appears where our hearts used to be, and the grief is real. *But it does not have to consume us.* As we lean on Him, Jesus will hold us up in this season.

⚒

Angie

I had heard about the empty nest when I was a young mom, but when your nest is full you can't comprehend an empty one. My nest began with one child and grew to seven.

The empty nest experience has been one of utter dependence upon God, a journey of trust and faith beyond sight. It's a flight into heights of pride in my children and their accomplishments and lows of self-doubt and fear.

Knowing the empty nest was looming from the day they were born, I sought to anchor my identity in Christ and not in my children, my job, or anything else. The emptying nest is lonely and disorienting, but it's taught me to perch on the branch of Him who holds me fast.

⚒

God gently reminded me, as He has countless times since, that He has a purpose in my pain, and He holds my daughter's life and future securely in His hands. He is holding your child, too.

> *The hardest days, when we choose trust instead of doubt, are the days that mold us, change us, and build our faith. – Kate*

Memories of days with our children may swirl through our minds, but fresh memories will unfold as we watch them march into their new and independent lives. We will discover that the experiences and opportunities not available when our children lived at home are suddenly perched squarely in front of us. But if we bind ourselves to the past, we risk missing the blessings around the next corner.

The key to surviving this season? Surrendering to the reality of what our lives are *now*. Failure to acknowledge this new reality can bruise us if we don't agree to it. You have invested your life as a mom and wife, but now, as you face an empty nest, what if God asks you to take on a new role, walk into a new calling, and dream a new future?

Will you say yes?

Mothering is a precious time in our lives ... but it is only half of our time on this earth.

Discussion Questions:

1. How would you describe yourself now ... a Robin, Mourning Dove, or Swallow mom?
2. What is your biggest fear about facing the empty nest?
3. What might be holding you back from surrendering your child's future to the Lord's care?
4. How can you begin to trust God with the transition from active mom to empty nester?
5. Do you believe God has your child's life firmly in His hands? How will you trust Him with their future ... and yours?
6. What are you most looking forward to in this new season?
7. What questions about your empty nest are keeping you up at night?

Scriptures:

- *In the multitude of my anxieties within me, Your comforts delight my soul.* Psalm 94:19
- *Be anxious for nothing, but in everything by prayer and supplication, with thanksgiving, let your requests be made known to God; and the peace of God, which surpasses all understanding, will guard your hearts and minds through Christ Jesus.* Philippians 4:6-7
- *Trust in the LORD with all your heart, And lean not on your own understanding; In all your ways acknowledge Him, And He shall direct your paths.* Proverbs 3:5-6
- *Have I not commanded you? Be strong and of good courage; do not be afraid, nor be dismayed, for the LORD your God is with you wherever you go.* Joshua 1:9
- *May the God of hope fill you with all joy and peace in believing, so that by the power of the Holy Spirit you may abound in hope.* Romans 15:13 (ESV)

A Prayer for Comfort

Lord, as my child leaves the nest, give me the strength to let go. I know You hold their lives and futures firmly in Your hands. As I enter this brand new and honestly, confusing phase, help me sort out all the unfamiliar emotions swirling through my mind.

I always knew that eventually I would face this "letting go" time, but it's much harder than I thought. Help me remember that You have designed and arranged a fresh chapter for me. As my children walk into the lives You have chosen, comfort my heart and soul as I release them into Your care, and at the same time, see my way forward into the future You have planned for me.

I ask for Your grace to embrace this next chapter with faith and courage. I trust Your plan for my life, wherever it may lead. As you fill the empty places in my heart with Your peace, I know that You are a good Father and that your love never wavers.

May Your word continually remind me of Your promises, as their truths anchor my soul to *Your* truth as I take my first steps into this new journey.

Motherhood is a beautiful gift, and I will *never* take it for granted. Thank You for the precious opportunity to raise the children You've given me. I ask that You grant me a renewed purpose as I jump into a fresh adventure with You. Thank You for guiding me with Your wisdom and sustaining me with your grace.

In Jesus' name,
Amen

CHAPTER 2

How Empty Nest Moms Face
A Change of Seasons

As the empty nest descends, loneliness plagues all three mama birds to some degree. I felt utterly isolated after my daughter left home. Because she was homeschooled and I was a stay-at-home mom, we spent lots of time together doing everything you can imagine. But now it hit me in one fell swoop that my first and primary purpose as a mom was over and done.

It felt like gazing through a solid glass window to a future just out of reach. I could almost touch it, but the hard glass blocked my grasp. I knew what I used to have, and I knew I didn't have it anymore ... *and I knew I could not get it back.* As all my priorities were rearranged in a nano-second, I was forced to acknowledge I now stood on the outside edge of everything, consigned to the margins of mothering.

It hurt, I was lonesome and confused by all the unexpected emotions churning around in my heart. Like all moms, I needed time to grieve, heal, and bounce back. As I did, I began eagerly anticipating the new opportunities awaiting me in this next season. It dawned on me ... this was *my choice.* I could either wrap my arms firmly around the future or languish in the past. The time had arrived to look *forward* and stop looking *back*.

God gave me permission to pivot. He gave me permission to dream. As my eyes opened to His truth, it became clearer that a world of opportunity was close at hand. Change takes courage. Perhaps an empty nest wasn't as bad as I'd been told. As time went on, I realized it was actually a *good* problem.

> *In a few decades, you will regret the opportunities you didn't seize more than the ones you did. Throw your net over the other side of the boat. Let the winds of adventure guide you. Navigate uncharted waters with an open heart and mind. As you embrace the unknown, you will find it holds the keys to deep growth and daring discovery.* – Kate

Our lives revamp when our children leave the nest. The first and most disquieting change can hit our emotions *hard*. Our kids have been the dominant attention-getting figures in our lives for nearly two decades, with both roles clearly defined. But now, parenting our grown children, we find ourselves in utterly uncharted territory.

∞

Terri

My son was always close to me, but he rightfully put his wife first after he got married. It took me a while to realize he was doing the right thing and to not feel rejected (dumb, since I had taught him to do just that!).

There's an old saying: "A son's a son till he takes a wife; A daughter's a daughter all of her life." (I have one of each.) The saying is true—be ready to give him to her and God. I never thought I'd be that mom, and it took me a while to see that I was!

❧

What impacts *them* impacts *us*. In fact, one day, you might become a grandmother which brings its own unique set of joys and trials. When that season arrives, you will find you are both the parent of your adult child *and* a grandparent. *And likely a mother-in-law.* All seasons and situations need to be addressed and managed differently.

A quick note about the season of grandparenting. Becoming a grandmother is a wonderful thing, *but it's not the only thing.* I posted about the empty nest on social media, and one of the women who commented thanked me for not making the role of grandmother the ultimate goal of the empty nest.

When others tell you that your empty nest will get better when you become a grandmother, yes, that might be true, but it's not guaranteed, and it's not certain to be in every mom's future. Some of your children may never marry, or can't have a child, or don't want to have a child, so for you, becoming a grandmother is out of the question. That doesn't diminish you one iota. God has much for you besides that.

We can't think the role of grandmother is our ultimate goal in life and the season that will solve our future. If it's in God's plan for you, wonderful. But if it's not, let God show you *His* plan, not the expectation others may assume.

Like a sudden summer thunderstorm, an onslaught of emotions can engulf us when our kids are grown and gone. Some of us, the Robin moms, will experience sadness and bittersweet joy. Even as precious memories flood our hearts, we also eagerly anticipate the future. Our Mourning Dove moms may face anxiety, worry, or depression descending out of nowhere. And the Swallow moms will be eager to move into the next phase, thirsty for what's on the horizon.

We may fret over the future and how to maintain strong relationships with our children as they head out to navigate their adult lives.

But we can't help wondering, does God have a new season for *me*, something perfectly designed, destined, and decided for *my* life? Is my mission behind me, over and done? Was being "mom" as good as it gets? You have invested your life as a wife and mom, but now, as you face your empty nest, God may be asking you to take on a brand-new role, walk into a new calling, and dream of an unexpected future with Him. Will you say yes?

Our kids are on their own, sometimes neglecting to call, making decisions and mistakes without any help from us, choosing the wrong friends, adulting by themselves, striving to make their mark in the world, and doing all they can to survive. God's perfect plan is for them to unfold life for themselves, even as they face every pitfall and temptation the world throws at them, just as we did.

But as much as we'd like to, we cannot hold their hands, even if they have abandoned their faith, descending into a lifestyle contrary to how they were raised. We are no longer the safe sanctuary where they can fail. They must create their own place now. *And we have to let go.*

Swallow Mom, you are thrilled to have the house to yourself...*finally.* And if you have more than one child, you might be enjoying a quiet and peaceful home for the first time! You have no trouble embracing this new-found freedom that has landed in your lap. You can explore new opportunities to walk fully into your calling as you watch your grocery bill and laundry pile shrink. The kitchen sink is empty, the utility bills are lower, the whole house stays cleaner longer, and there are no more sibling fights to referee.

The best part? Relishing how your children are growing and maturing as they handle life on their own, cheering them on as you watch them fly. We have the great privilege to witness their character blossom as they practice the precepts we modeled during our years of parenting, and we can stand back, watching proudly as they become the men and women of God He created them to be.

Shawna

I am a married mom. My husband and I enjoy doing things alone and having less laundry to do was a nice benefit. However, these positives also came with feelings of guilt. It's such a strange stage of life.

One of the things I've said, along with friends going through the same thing, is that no one talks about what it's like, so you're blindsided by all the feelings.

I experienced a time of mourning. The loss of what was and knowing it would never be the same while being excited for my children to make their own way in the world. I also experienced fear for them going out into the world on their own, more so for my daughter than my son. I'm still heavily involved in my kid's lives, but not the same way anymore.

⊱∾⊰

Discussion Questions:

1. What emotions are you dealing with right now in your empty nest journey?
2. Do you have an idea of what your next season holds? What is it?
3. What parts of the empty nest are you beginning to enjoy?
4. Are you doubting your future? What can you do to change that?

Scriptures:

- *And the LORD will guide you continually and satisfy your desire in scorched places and make your bones strong; and you shall be like a watered garden, like a spring of water, whose waters do not fail. Isaiah 58:11 (ESV)*
- *Draw near to God and He will draw near to you.* James 4:8
- *Fear not, for I am with you; be not dismayed, for I am your God. I will strengthen you, Yes, I will help you, I will uphold you with my righteous right hand. Isaiah 41:10*
- *I can do all things through Christ who strengthens me.* Philippians 4:13

A Prayer for Doubt

Lord, I'm not sure about my future, my worth, my purpose, or pretty much everything in my life as I face these uncharted waters of the empty nest. I'm doing my best to navigate this new and intimidating season. I'm lonelier that I thought I'd be, and some days are hard to get through.

You have a purpose for the rest of my life. I'm seeking clarity for my next steps. The hardest part is understanding who I am now that my children have grown and gone. Please help me to discern what direction You would have me take.

Give me the patience needed to wait for You to move and direct my footsteps. Only You know what is best for my future and the proper path for my life. I don't want to assume that I know the direction for the next stage You've designed for me. and I don't ever want to rush ahead of Your plan for me. Let me hear Your voice and direction during this in-between time, this season of uncertainty.

Thank You for guiding my every footstep.

In Jesus' name,

Amen

CHAPTER 3

Seasons Season *Us*

We will each experience a variety of seasons over a lifetime. Seasons of fullness or loss, purpose or emptiness, mourning or dancing. As they ebb and flow, I have found it fruitless to fight the one I'm in. I can no more change it than I can make an icy winter melt into spring.

I hate waiting at red lights, getting stuck behind slowpokes in the left lane, waiting for the bread to rise or for the dryer to finish its cycle. I'm eager for the class to end, the food to cook, and the leaves to change. Getting to the next part, the "better part" makes me anxious to move into the next season—except when it came time to step into my empty nest.

> *It's in the waiting that the test comes, and the test is how we handle the wait.* – Kate

When our children are babies, we're thrilled to see them take their first steps as we impatiently anticipate the next milestone. We're eager to skip past the delay and drop anchor at the *next* milestone. But that isn't how it works. God wants us to practice patience, thankfulness, and learning to rest in who He *is*, not merely what He *gives*.

We get so focused on the future that we can quickly become frustrated in the present. I sometimes find it hard to be thankful and am easily annoyed when what I am waiting for does not show up according to my timeline.

But if things are not changing or moving fast enough, there is a reason.

During this season, we can learn to press in where we are and worry less about where we are going. There is a good chance many of us won't be so encumbered with obligations and commitments, family needs, and social events as we are right now. Our job? Enjoy what is in our hands *now*. Find satisfaction today. This might frustrate some of you Robin or Swallow mamas, but as the word teaches us in Acts 10:34, God is no respecter of persons, meaning He never shows favoritism, He's impartial. If we are following Jesus, most if not all of us will be required to wait patiently at some point in our After Party.

Are you like me and find it hard to wait…to be still…to do nothing? Waiting forces us to remain in the moment.

I've battled the seasons in my life, and I bet you have too. As God has required me to press through each one, He has revealed ten truths about seasons during four decades of walking with Him.

1. *Enjoy the now.* By their very nature, seasons change, arriving whether we want them to or not, and they seem to disappear like a gentle morning mist the moment we become comfortable. Let's do our best to enjoy what we can in our current season.

2. *We are learning lessons,* no matter what it looks like—even if it's a waiting season. *Especially* if it's a waiting season. God is teaching us something in the delay. If we press in and listen, we might hear Him speak. Maybe He wants us to want *Him* more than whatever we might be waiting for.

   Delay isn't the end of your story. – Kate

3. *Be thankful for the seasons we're in*—even the hard ones. Hard ones come, and we will not always understand why He puts us in uncomfortable seasons, but God has a purpose in our pain. We cannot always fathom His intent. My best advice? Give thanks in everything.
4. *The waiting is a test.* We can press in and learn from it or push against it and experience much frustration.
5. *God is in no hurry.* The more we try to elbow in and manipulate the current season, the longer it may last.
6. *The training teaches us to rest where we are.* Sometimes, as Psalm 23 says, God *makes us lie down.*
7. *Don't rush past the now moments.* Days will come when gratitude has slipped our grasp, and we cannot see one. good. thing. It's like walking down a dimly lit and crooked path with no end in sight. But as we open our eyes and contemplate our position with a *grateful heart,* the dust clears, the light shines, and we will recognize much to appreciate in the current season.
8. *Find the blessing in today.* Whatever Jesus is teaching us will move with us into the next season. It

all has a point because, ultimately, His goal is to make us *more like Him.*

9. *Learn to wait quietly.* To be still and know... taking time away from the computer/cell phone/ social media distractions to connect with Christ and those around us. Real life, face to face.

10. *Let the season you are in season you.* And share what you are learning. It might surprise you to find out that you are not alone as you discover how many of your friends are going through the same life challenges.

Change can be unsettling, and not all seasons are fun, easy, or guaranteed to bring happiness. But difficult seasons have taught me this: God is not after my happiness but my highest good. I am certain that, by their very nature, the season WILL change.

So, hang in there!

Seasons Come and Seasons Go

To everything there is a season, A time
for every purpose under heaven.
Ecclesiastes 3:1-8

Strong's Concordance translates the Hebrew word we know as *season* (Strong's #2165) as an appointed occasion or time. So, to everything, there is an appointed time, which illustrates a process, events happening in an orderly fashion appointed by God in the wisdom of His will.

There are multiple seasons mentioned in Ecclesiastes, twenty-eight in fact. No wonder it seems life continues to shift and adjust!

To everything there is a season,
A time for every purpose under heaven:
A time to be born, And a time to die;
A time to plant, And a time to pluck what is planted;
A time to kill, And a time to heal;
A time to break down, And a time to build up;
A time to weep, And a time to laugh;
A time to mourn, And a time to dance;
A time to cast away stones, And a time to gather stones;
A time to embrace, And a time to refrain from embracing;
A time to gain, And a time to lose;
A time to keep, And a time to throw away;
A time to tear, And a time to sew;
A time to keep silence, And a time to speak;
A time to love, And a time to hate;
A time of war, And a time of peace.
Ecclesiastes 3:1-8

Many of these seasons deeply resonate with me regarding the empty nest. Times like, *"A time to mourn, and a time to dance… A time to gain, and a time to lose… A time to keep silent, and a time to speak… A time to tear, and a time to sew."*

Our Mourning Dove moms will experience grief as their children move on, but as they step into their next adventure, they will find their own opportunity to dance, to gain, to speak, to sew. At times, our seasons appear to be overturned and mixed up. We are not sure which one we're in and which comes next. But hear these tender words in verse eleven, *He has made everything beautiful in its time.*

My heart calms as I read this line, and I marvel at God's plan, His provision, and His providence.

The Father artfully choreographs each one of His
appointed times and seasons for our lives. – Kate

✤

Kristi

I was a stay-at-home mom (part-time job), and when the oldest was going into high school, I realized I needed something to occupy my time besides my kids.

I never finished my nursing degree so off I went. I was scared to death to step back inside college doors at age 40, but I did. I made some of the best friends and still have them!

My kids all graduated and went to college (I graduated from college the same year as my son). Still, the empty nest hit me hard.

I have a husband who was totally supportive, but it was just hard, and I went on anti-anxiety meds to help me through it and questioned why my faith wasn't big enough to handle it all.

Goodness! I have a lump in my throat just remembering everything that happened.

Fast forward to today. My kids are all married, live within an hour of us, and we have been blessed with 10 grandkids!

✤

We will experience most, if not all, of these twenty-eight seasons. Like a wandering river, our lives are fluid and ever-changing. As soon as we grow accustomed to the heat of summer, the whisper of fall hovers in the air. Leaves begin to change, and days get shorter as the air turns refreshingly cool…with winter's chill right around the corner. As parents, the empty nest season brings new joys *and* challenges to understand and contend with.

You can be certain of this—when you have a handle on one season, it may very well change. Some last longer than others, and some will surprise us as they propel us forward with ferocious speed. There are those causing us to grow and others requiring us to put into practice what we learned in the previous season. We leapfrog over some of them entirely. But the majority of empty nest moms will experience a large proportion of them.

Discussion Questions:

1. What emotions have you dealt with as you have faced (or will soon face) your empty nest?
2. How are you learning to live in the hard place in your empty nest?
3. What can you do to *lean not on your own understanding?* Proverbs 3:5-6
4. What season do you think you are in, from Ecclesiastes 3:1-8?
5. As you look back on the different seasons of motherhood, which one has been the best and most rewarding, and which has been the hardest?
6. Are you learning to press in where you are, or worrying about where you're going? How can you work on that?

Scriptures:

- *And let us not grow weary while doing good, for in due season we shall reap if we do not lose heart.* Galatians 6:9
- *You have set all the borders of the earth; You have made summer and winter.* Psalms 74:17

- *... being confident of this very thing, that He who has begun a good work in you will complete it until the day of Jesus Christ.* Philippians 1:6
- *... knowing that the testing of your faith produces patience.* James 1:3
- *He makes me to lie down in green pastures; He leads me beside the still waters.*
  Psalm 23:2

Prayer to Trust

Father, so many thoughts are swirling through my mind right now, but I know You know them all. I'm sitting here staring at a brand-new, mysterious season filled with transition and change, and I'm not at all certain what the future holds for me. But I know You do.

I trust You, and I pray for Your strength to help me stretch my boundaries. Show me how to walk boldly into the life You have chosen for me. I give You everything I have because You alone know the future and the plans You have prepared for me. I am forever grateful that You hear, love, and protect me.

Give me wisdom to navigate this new season with grace and patience, helping me to lean on You for guidance and support. May Your peace, which surpasses all understanding, guard my heart and mind in Christ Jesus.

Lord, I know I can do all things through Christ, who gives me strength. I place my trust in You, knowing that You are faithful to uphold me and to lead me onward, step by step, as I begin this journey of the empty nest.

In Jesus' name,
Amen

CHAPTER 4

Many Empty Nest Moms Are Saying: "What Do I Do with All My Time?"

Whether we're working moms or stay-at-home moms, once our kids are out of the house, many of us will have more hours to call our own and, likely, a bit more breathing room. We still need to take care of all the routine daily tasks (cooking, cleaning, laundry, etc.), but many other tasks will evaporate.

Imagine not having to create a detailed spreadsheet or weekly task list for all those school projects and homework assignments. What freedom to no longer have to figure out who needs to be where when, and how on earth to get them there! For working moms, the constant need to balance work and parenting has changed. For all of us, our work of mothering has seriously downsized.

Many moms are deliriously grateful for a little more time in the evenings than normal. Maybe they've juggled a part-time or full-time job around parenting, and the extra time is a wonderful side benefit, even as the rest of their schedule remains largely the same as they head out to their normal workday. But many other moms wrestle with how to turn the new empty hours into something meaningful.

We're supposed to "keep busy," right? My husband, who spent most of our marriage working *from* home, was now working *outside* of the home, so I was alone a lot. My time was suddenly all mine ... *and I had no idea what to do with it.*

I love to cook, so after my daughter left home, I started a food blog called *The Kitchen Princess.* Lame, I know, but it served its purpose during those years after our daughter moved to Nashville. I wanted her to have easy access to all the recipes she loved ... like my homemade chili, chicken noodle soup, carrot cake, and most of all, her dad's famous meatballs and spaghetti. I needed somewhere to put all the recipes, and a blog felt like the perfect fit.

As my blog and readership grew, I felt impressed to share more posts about living a godly life and walking with the Lord. My byline? *Food, Faith, and Family.* Though I was writing, I never once considered myself a "writer." I simply wrote what was on my heart, hoping readers would find my blog and enjoy it. Writing helped a bit, but it couldn't fully satisfy the aching loneliness. I had absolutely no idea of the unpredictable plan God had up His sleeve for my future.

God dared me to write a book when I wasn't a writer. I knew I *could* write. It simply never entered my mind to write a book. It was not even in my vocabulary!

Little did I know Jesus was about to transform my life and purpose permanently and unexpectedly just as I tried to find my balance and come to grips with my empty nest.

God stood me up, turned me around, and, out of the blue, brought something brand new into my life … smack dab in the middle of my empty nest.

Here's how it happened.

One night, I received a call from the lady who ran the homeschooling organization we had been part of. She invited my husband and me to speak to the parents at their big twentieth-anniversary celebration. She asked us to share the steps we took to raise our daughter to become a godly young woman who was able to find and walk into her calling, all while maintaining her relationship with the Lord.

The anniversary event was happening in a few weeks and the host was eager to have the parents hear what Mike and I had to say. Hesitatingly, I said yes … but honestly, I didn't know *what* we would talk about. We certainly weren't poster children for how to parent perfectly.

By this point, Francesca had moved to Nashville, signed a record deal, released her first CD, had hit songs on the radio, and was beginning to have name recognition.

After I hung up the phone, I turned to my husband and asked him what we *had* done. As we discussed it, we discovered we had been far more intentional in raising her than we realized. Together we came up with fifteen specific actions we had taken to raise her with strong biblical principles, modeling a passionate love for the Lord. Two weeks later, we gave our talk to an eager audience.

The morning after our talk, as I prayed and thanked the Lord for those fifteen things, I sensed the

Lord speak in my spirit, telling me that they were book chapters. It's what I call a *God Dare*. Taken completely off-guard, I gave Him every excuse I could think of to say no.

I haven't heard God speak so clearly very many times in my life, but as His words resonated in my spirit, I *knew* it was Him. I gave Him numerous excuses for why I could *never* write a book.

- I was not a trained writer.
- I didn't have a college degree *(though I did go to four colleges in two years and didn't graduate from any of them… but that's another story altogether!)*.
- I reminded Him I was not a parenting expert.
- I had no platform, and no one would publish it, and on and on.

I tried every way but sideways *not* to do what He was telling me to do. But as His words echoed through my mind, it became crystal clear that I had no valid excuse.

What did I do? I said yes to God's dare. He knows me better than I know myself, and He knows what I am capable of. I also knew that if He called me to it, He would have to equip me to do it because, to my mind at least, I couldn't even *think* about writing a book. Isn't it amazing how things change when we step out with God and watch Him do the impossible?

Debbie

When my last child went to college, I spontaneously pulled into a music store, rented a violin, and signed up for lessons.

My husband still worked long hours. The violin gave me something to focus on each day.

I started with classical violin, then switched to mostly Irish fiddling. The gift was in filling long hours and bonding with my violin and two amazing teachers.

᙮

As I have grown in my walk with the Lord, I realize that if God dares us, success (as He measures it) is guaranteed if we take Him at His word, trust, follow, and believe. If He dares us to do it, He knows we *can* do it. But only if we believe He believes in us.

I flew past every single excuse I had given Him. Well, except for the four colleges in two years. I couldn't change that. But I did what God dared me to do, and I wrote my first book, *Growing Great Kids: Partner with God to Cultivate His Purpose in Your Child's Life*. And it was published!

Here's the thing, girls: If God calls you to it, He *will* equip you to do it. And if God tells you to do it, anything is possible. In fact, as I say in my second book, *The God Dare*: "The impossible is God's comfort zone."

> *Whether you think you can or you think*
> *you can't, you're right.* – Kate

Is God daring you to reach for what you believe are unattainable goals? Do you sense He's calling you to something new and unfamiliar in this curious empty nest season? Has He given you unprecedented pockets of time, but you sense He has specific intentions for them?

Ultimately, it is our choice to obey. We are free to say no and stay shut up in our little happy/miserable places. But we can push through fear and follow His lead. We might not know where we will end up, but if He instructs us to move forward, He will lead us on the right path.

Sometimes we choose our paths, and other times, our paths are chosen for us. Each day holds a future we are yet to meet.

I had a choice to make the moment He dared me. I could limit myself, ignore the still, small Voice, settle for less, and stay safe. But I didn't. I pushed through my fear and umpteen excuses. And now I can officially call myself by a new name. *Author and speaker.*

Change takes courage. – Kate

What is He daring you to do? Maybe your passion is counseling in a pro-life clinic or working at your local homeless shelter. Can you imagine what it would be like to get your college degree or start your own business? Have you always wanted to work with seniors in a memory care unit at your local hospital or run for office? There are as many paths as there are people!

Discussion Questions:

1. Have you ever felt challenged to do something bigger than you thought you could accomplish? What was it?
2. How did that make you feel, and how did you contend with it?
3. Where do you believe God is calling you in your next season?

4. Will you obey regardless of what God calls you to, or are you struggling?
5. God wants us to dream big with Him. How can you begin to do that today?

Scriptures:

- *... be it unto me according to thy word.* Luke 1:38 (KJV)
- *You will keep him in perfect peace, whose mind is stayed on You, because he trusts in You.* Isaiah 26:3
- *My frame was not hidden from You, when I was made in secret, and skillfully wrought in the lowest parts of the earth. Your eyes saw my substance, being yet unformed. And in Your book they all were written, the days fashioned for me, when as yet there were none of them.* Psalm 139:15-16
- *The steps of a good man are ordered by the LORD, and He delights in his way.* Psalm 37:23

A Prayer for Courage

Father, it's a brand-new season and my heart is full. I'm excited for what the future may hold, but I still have uncertainties and questions.

I'm apprehensive about my next steps. But, as 2 Timothy 1:7 assures me, You haven't given me a spirit of fear but of power and love and a sound mind. Fill me afresh with courage and the ability to face this new phase with boldness and confidence.

Let me see my empty nest as an opportunity for growth and breakthrough, not a time of confusion, loss, or despair. I ask for boldness to step into the new possibilities You are giving me. Teach me how to give wings to my dreams and passions that have been dormant for years.

I need clarity of vision to see the path ahead, even if it's only for the very next step. Remind me of Your great and precious promises and who I am in You.

You alone are my rock and my refuge, and I am leaning fully on You for wisdom. I trust You, Father, and I know You will give me the courage I need to walk fully into my destiny. I know You planned my life before the foundation of the world.

In Jesus' name,
Amen

CHAPTER 5

MANY EMPTY NEST MOMS AGREE: THE AFTER PARTY IS *GOOD*

O ur Swallow moms are thrilled to have more free time on hand to pursue their passions and focus on their interests or hobbies. Robin moms may feel some trepidation as they dispatch their children into the world, yet they are content having raised strong, independent, godly children who can face life with boldness and confidence. Mourning Dove moms might need a little push to move into this new season.

Why? What makes the After Party so special for some of us?

For one ... it's exciting.

Lots of moms eagerly anticipate this new era, joyfully embracing their newfound freedom once their kids have flown the coop. They have a plan and can see their next step. They are prepared for this season, ready to plunge in. But they too may be asking, "What's next?"

Now is our moment to find out who we are, mama. It is our chance to rediscover ourselves, dust off the

47

dreams and visions we buried years ago and give them wings. It is time to stomp fear on the head and plunge in!

✖

Kristy

I have three kids. Two daughters are in college—freshman and sophomore this year. We have a son who will be a senior in high school. I'd say that I felt some relief when they left, and they did well, made friends, and passed their classes.

I love it when they come home, but I'm usually ready for them to get back to school. Is that bad? I don't think so, but I don't freely share my thoughts because some moms say an empty nest feels like grief.

✖

We had years when our primary objective was raising our family. But children grow up, and that stage abruptly ends. They all grow and go, and we know from the beginning this is the script we are following. As we approach that unavoidable future, we understand in theory that a new season is headed our way... *but that does not make it any easier.*

It's Curtain Up on Act II.

God is daring us to strike out and discover more purpose, more prospects, and more adventure than we ever thought possible. This is not the end of our story by any means. God may have dropped a dream in your heart years ago. A little seed that has germinated, begun to grow, ready to emerge from the ground, be fed, and flourish. During our After Parties, we can rediscover what we love and begin to let go of what might be holding us back from our futures.

Or your experience may be more like mine. I had *no idea* what God had in store for me. He might have an entirely new path for you, too, with a trajectory you never saw coming.

One huge benefit of the After Party is this: We have more time to press in and grow closer than ever to Jesus. Our time is our own, providing us fresh opportunities to dig deep, putting down rich roots in our relationship with Him. We have extra freedom to learn the Word and expanded time to sit in His presence and hear what He has to say to us. Many of us now have more time to join a neighborhood Bible study or volunteer for a ministry.

*Intimacy with Jesus will blossom the
more you tend it.* – Kate

Who Does *He* Say You Are?

God placed in each of us the capacity to change the world with our lives. He designed us *with* a purpose and *for* a purpose that was formed before the foundation of the world. As it says in Jeremiah: *"Before I formed you in the womb I knew you; Before you were born I sanctified you; I ordained you a prophet to the nations"* (Jeremiah 1:5). Whether we have been set apart for fame and fortune or a life of obscurity and selfless service in the trenches, our lives can transform the atmosphere around us, impacting the world. We are part of something so much bigger than ourselves.

> *We might believe our empty nests are a crisis*
> *when, in truth, they are pure opportunities*
> *to discover other paths and God's design*
> *for the second half of our lives.* – Kate

In Romans 2:11, we are reminded that God *shows no partiality.* We all like our safe spaces, our comfortable surroundings, and the sense of security they afford. But God has a way of calling us out of our safe and secure situations, as He gently shepherds us into the realm of complete trust.

You cannot offend God with a big dream. He is not sitting back thinking, *who does she think she is?* No. He expects and wants us to let our imaginations fly trusting Him alone as we approach this next phase of life. He asks us to step out and step into the life He planned for us before the foundation of the world.

And it does not matter what we may have done in the past. It can hold so many of us back because we wrongly assume God can't use us because we "messed up too much."

Mama, if you have repented and asked God to forgive you, then the only things holding you back are your own excuses. It is easy to park yourself in the lie that you are not worthy or that God cannot use you. That is the devil's dare to keep you *exactly* where he wants you. Don't fall for it. Go all in for your future. God designed it *just for you.*

Let me ask you this one critical question: *Can you trust God with your future?* Will you say yes to His plan for your life? Does Jesus get to pick what your next season will bring? Will you trust Him and agree with the life He chooses for you? Who does *He* say you are?

Discussion Questions:

1. Do you believe God has a purpose and a future for you beyond motherhood?
2. If so, what do you think it is?
3. Will you trust Him with it? If not, why not?
4. How do you see God beginning to shape you for your next phase (like me writing a recipe blog, which led to writing a book)?
5. How will you let Jesus pick your next season?

Scriptures:

- *Be strong and courageous. Do not fear or be in dread of them, for it is the* LORD *your God who goes with you. He will not leave you or forsake you.* Deuteronomy 31:6 (ESV)
- *Many are the plans in the mind of a man, but it is the purpose of the* LORD *that will stand.* Proverbs 19:21 (ESV)
- *And we know that all things work together for good to those who love God, to those who are the called according to His purpose.* Romans 8:28
- *For we are His workmanship, created in Christ Jesus for good works, which God prepared beforehand that we should walk in them.* Ephesians 2:10

A Prayer for the Future

Father, my heart overflows with anticipation as I glimpse the path ahead. I know You know the plans You have for me, and I am eager to walk into them fearlessly. Help me have the courage to dream a big, impossible dream with You.

Open my eyes to new opportunities and give me the boldness I need for the next step. Remind me of the gifts and talents You've given me for the purpose of changing the world around me for Your great name.

I need discernment every day to hear Your voice alone and not the voice of any other. Let all my choices align with Your will for my life, and if they don't, close those doors. Let the Holy Spirit be my constant companion, guiding me every step of the way and protecting me from harm and wrong decisions. With You, I know I can do all things.

Lord, I surrender my plans to You. Your ways are far higher than mine and I want only Your will to be done in my life. I trust You for your provision, guidance, and faithfulness.

In Jesus' name,
Amen

THE CHALLENGE

CHAPTER 6

MANY EMPTY NEST MOMS SAY: THE AFTER PARTY IS *HARD*

When our children leave home, both Mourning Dove and Robin moms can sink into a season of sadness, despondency, anxiety, gloom, or self-pity, topped off by a profound sense of loss. Here's a crazy idea...what if we do this instead? What if we take our empty nest opportunity to explore exactly what the Lord has for us *today?*

God is not done with us simply because our active role in raising children has passed. As confusing as this new life stage might be, He has far more for us to discover about ourselves and our mission than we can even begin to fathom. What is God daring you to do in this season...your own personal *God dare?*

Now is a perfect time to journal all those feelings. Emotions swirl as we begin to ponder our future. What ideas do we have for Act 2 of Motherhood? What thoughts need to be taken captive (2 Corinthians 10:5)? There are ample scriptures providing guidance, teaching us how to handle everything from anxiety and sorrow to grief and loneliness.

Many will encourage us as we walk through this season. We can dig into those that speak to our hearts, reminding us of what God's word says about our situation. Writing our thoughts and feelings down offers a soul-refreshing opportunity to explore and clarify exactly what is churning around in our hearts. As we do, it will give clarity as we talk to God about it.

The empty nest experience affects each of us differently, but it *does* affect all of us. You are not alone, and if you have supportive friends, especially friends who have been empty nesters for a while, spend time with them so they can help you process your pain.

Do you know an older woman who has been in her After Party for a few years? Check in with her and ask for counsel and advice. She has already weathered the transition and gained her equilibrium in this new reality and can encourage you that this season *is* survivable.

Depending on lots of factors, most of us will experience a combination of emotions. The age of our children, our other personal circumstances (single mom, stay-at-home mom, working mom, disabled mom, etc.) or if we have additional pressing responsibilities, such as caring for a physically challenged child or aging parents, or a disability of our own.

Also important is the kind of relationship we have with our children. Are we on good terms, or is the relationship strained with no communication at all? We all face a unique mix of circumstances as our children leave the nest.

☙

Joan

I had a terrible time when my last little fledgling went off to college one month short of her 18th birthday. She was still in our same town but chose to move in with her BFF in an apartment near campus.

I cried and cried. I didn't know what to do with myself since being a "Mom" to my two girls was my job for quite a while. It took me some time to get over the feeling of despair. Am I completely over it? No. It's been over 20 years now, and I still miss them as much or more as they live in other cities now.

As much as we would like to oversee every decision our kids make, it's time to come to terms with this tough truth: they *can* survive without us. We can stay as involved in their lives and as connected as possible, but it is imperative that we resist becoming hovering, "helicopter moms." Give them the chance to spread their wings and fly. *Our love should never be a prison.*

If we try to mend *them*, it may break *us*.

Communicate with them regularly, visit occasionally, offer advice rarely *(unless they ask)*, and let them know how proud you are of their accomplishments and how well they are handling life on their own.

Open communication with our kids is key. We must remain steadfastly honest about our values and expectations and listen, listen, listen to what they have to say! Disagree when appropriate. Empathize when needed. Redirect stray ideas. And above all, stay in consistent contact with your child as much as you are able.

Then let them live their lives. If they make mistakes and fail, be there to help as the Lord leads, but remember ... *failure is a great teacher.*

Be as available as they need you to be, even if it isn't convenient. As they open up, our kids will share their struggles and fears, joys and accomplishments, hopes, heartaches, and grief. They do truly still need us...just in a different way. Remember, they are in a brand-new stage of life, too.

We Are Not Them

One more thing to ponder, mama. *We are not him or her.* Our personalities may be very different from our own moms...as we all likely discovered during our teenage years!

I mentioned in chapter one that my daughter and I have decidedly distinct and different personalities. I am a fixer and a problem solver. In my mind, there is one correct way to handle a situation—*my* way. Needless to say, that does not bear healthy fruit. I had to learn to relate to her differently than my normal, go-to style.

Over time, I determined to parent who *she* is, and remember *she is not me.* Sometimes, I was not able to resolve her issue, which was okay because she needed her mom to be a listener not a fixer.

Our children must eventually figure life out for themselves. We cannot pick them up when they fall, solve every problem, or remove every one of life's inevitable obstacles from their path. And I think that particularly applies to parents of only children (more than twenty percent of families and is expected to double by 2050).

Roberta
Empty nesting is a huge transition for parents as they let go of full control of their children. We just have to pray that God

will send His angels to watch over and protect them when they are no longer in our care. All the ups and downs, achievements and failures, sadness and joy, depression and acceleration are all there to build our endurance and resilience as parents.

We do the best we know how at the time… nobody gives you directions on how to raise your children. We do our best, and let God do the rest!

We can become so wrapped up in our child's life that we lose focus on other important matters in our own lives. Parents of only children may run the risk of turning them into a singular obsession or an idol. When that's the case, their transition into the empty nest stage can be an even more turbulent one.

Your experience is unique to you. Be patient with yourself and know that, over time, you will adjust to this new stage of life, find your mission, and discover new ways to flourish.

Many Mourning Dove moms battle grief big time, and the sense of loss can be palpable. Emotions can drag us all over the place like an out-of-control ping-pong ball batted about by some unseen hand. We may find ourselves completely out of sync with life as we've always known it.

Life will challenge us, but amid the challenges,
God will give us wings to rise above the heartache
as we discover a bigger picture. – Kate

The good news is, as the Lord helps us work through the confusion, the grief will ease and eventually dissipate, no longer hijacking our lives. In fact, joy will return as we experience and celebrate our kids, watching them flourish. We can move forward into our new calling as After Party survivors and find our sense of grief beginning to ebb.

Mourning Dove moms, now that you've begun your After Party, have you ever found yourself in your kitchen looking forlornly into your fridge or pantry for something to eat, only to sadly realize you no longer have any idea what to make for dinner?

The frozen pizza and chicken nuggets are gone, all the snacks and sodas have disappeared, and you have *no clue* what to cook. For the first time, maybe in years, you can actually see the back of your pantry... only to find jars and boxes you had completely forgotten about, most of them way past the "sell by" date.

It's clear your kids have moved on, and though it may cause momentary sadness, you can now fill your fridge and pantry with whatever *you* want to eat... and keep it much less cluttered in the bargain! As you recognize this new truth, a faint smile begins to form. It becomes apparent that maybe the empty nest isn't such a bad thing after all...

Discussion Questions:

1. Are emotions overwhelming you right now? What are you doing to cope with them?
2. How do you think journaling your feelings might help?
3. How would you describe your relationship with your children in this season?

4. In what ways has your relationship with your children changed?
5. What positives are you beginning to recognize in your empty nest?

Scriptures:

- *Peace I leave with you, My peace I give to you; not as the world gives do I give to you. Let not your heart be troubled, neither let it be afraid.* John 14:27
- *You will show me the path of life; In Your presence is fullness of joy; At Your right hand are pleasures forevermore.* Psalm 16:11
- *Come to Me, all you who labor and are heavy laden, and I will give you rest.* Matthew 11:28
- *See, I have inscribed you on the palms of My hands.* Isaiah 49:16
- *We demolish arguments and every pretension that sets itself up against the knowledge of God, and we take captive every thought to make it obedient to Christ.* 2 Corinthians 10:5 (NIV)

A Prayer for Acceptance

Lord, I'm doing my best not to slip into depression or self-pity, but it's hard. Memories of days with my children give me some comfort but also can send me into deep pits of regret and loneliness.

I realize I can't control their lives the way I used to. Please help me resist the urge to advise when I'm not asked. Remind me to listen and keep communication open at all times, even when it's inconvenient.

Remind me that my children can survive without me. My identity has been wrapped up with theirs for so long, it can be hard to acknowledge that my role has changed.

I'm thrilled to watch them fly into their new lives and eager to cheer them on, but who is cheering *me* on? I know You are always with me. I am eager to sense Your presence in a new and fresh way in this unfamiliar and daunting stage of life. Teach me to accept what I can't change.

In Jesus' name,
Amen

CHAPTER 7

THREE TRUTHS TO HELP YOU
COPE WITH YOUR EMPTY NEST

I tend to wallow in self-pity…what my husband calls "my favorite bad feeling." He is completely right, but I wallow anyway. And my Mourning Dove self wallowed aggressively when our daughter left home…until it became clear that I had to leave my pity party and do something, *anything*. Did I want to be pitiful or powerful, victor or victim?

Starting my little food blog was God's sneaky way of getting me to write. After our daughter got married and started giving us grandchildren, it dawned on me that I had been at the After Party for quite a while.

Most of us are likely to face certain predictable realities in the early part of the empty nest. I wish someone had shared a few truths with me before my little nest emptied.

It can be worrisome.

We worry about the future, how our kids will fare in the world, and how we will maintain a strong relationship with them as they begin their adult lives. Watching our children grow up and leave home can be a bitter-sweet exercise of endurance seasoned with a big dose of trust.

It is normal to feel forlorn and nostalgic as we look back to the years when they needed us for every single thing, every single day. But remember this: *we are raising them to go.* We are raising them to find their own path. It is their chance to discover God's roadmap to adult-hood and what He has in store for them *without us.*

It's deafeningly quiet.

If you have become accustomed to lots of noise in your home—like the kids clamoring for breakfast early in the morning, shouts of "Mom, I need help with my homework!" or wrangling everyone in for dinner—it is suddenly quieter than you have known in years. It is unnerving, to say the least.

But on the flip side, you will find your home cleaner and less cluttered, and your grocery bill will be much, much lower—especially if you have boys! Swallow moms, in particular, will enjoy the freedom perched right before them.

Robin moms may wander aimlessly around their homes, ending up in the mysteriously cleared out laun-dry room. The hamper is completely empty, and she stares at it in awestruck wonder, feeling both relief and heartache. She ponders her newfound freedom, and may very well waltz out of the room, realizing she's been set free from those endless piles of dirty clothes!

It's lonely.

We've spent years with our kids, and it is no sur-prise that we feel isolated and alone when they are gone. If you're the mom of an only child, it's especially easy to feel the full weight of the *empty* in the empty nest.

Oh, and did I mention perimenopause and menopause? Just as our lives are turning upside down, our bodies are beginning to change, too. Sorry to remind you, but that is likely to hit in the next couple of years if it hasn't already.

I don't know why God allowed menopause to clobber us just as we are letting our kids go, but He did. A lot of the symptoms are the same. Sleep troubles due to either hormones or excessive worrying, right? Bursting into tears at the slightest memory or as we walk past their room or notice all the smelly sneakers have disappeared. Stress eating. Anxiety. Panic attacks as we face uncertain futures. Hot flashes. Confusion and crabbiness.

But I will leave that right there.

At the same time, although the empty nest and menopause may not be the serene journey you had hoped for, both are filled with many moments of growth, joy, and unexpected beauty. We're reaching the midway point of our lives, but remember your story and your future is only half-told.

The best part of a play is the second half. – Kate

We cannot and should not deny our emotions. They are real and powerful. But let's not allow them to swoop in, taking over our future and hijacking our peace. If we hand our loneliness to Jesus, He will give us *His* peace, guidance, and a path forward to our future.

Discussion Questions:

1. What emotions are you feeling as you settle into your empty nest?
2. Are you worrying about your kids? What can you do that might help you stop worrying?
3. How are you dealing with the loneliness?
4. What tools do you have to combat grief and anxiety?
5. How are you able to keep open communication with your children?
6. Are you concerned about wasting some of the additional time you've been given? How much time do you spend on social media each day? What steps can you take to limit it?

Scriptures:

- *But those who wait on the LORD shall renew their strength. They shall mount up with wings like eagles. They shall run and not be weary. They shall walk and not faint.* Isaiah 40:31
- *He heals the brokenhearted and binds up their wounds.* Psalm 147:3
- *Why are you cast down, O my soul, and why are you in turmoil within me? Hope in God; for I shall again praise him my salvation.* Psalm 42:5 (ESV)
- *For I will pour water on him who is thirsty, and floods on the dry ground. I will pour My Spirit on your descendants, and My blessing on your offspring. They will spring up among the grass like willows by the watercourses.* Isaiah 44:3-4

A Prayer for Peace

Father, You know my heart is heavy with loneliness and longing as I walk through this new stage in my mothering journey. The silence outshines the laughter that once filled my home, and I miss the life that used to bubble over with activity and purpose every day. But You are the God of peace, a peace that passes my understanding.

I ask that You wash me in Your presence today, ministering to my heart and comforting me by reminding me of Your unfailing love. Prompt me to seek fellowship with the friends and loved ones who will encourage and support me. Help me share what I'm going through with trusted friends.

Teach me to find contentment in You alone, as You are the source of all true peace and fulfillment. I ask that Your peace will guard my heart and my mind and keep me from falling into anxiety and despair as it fills me with hope and confidence in Your goodness.

I place every bit of my loneliness and longing into Your hands. I trust that You are working out my future in Your way and perfect timing, because You work all things for my good. I know You alone are able to bring joy from heartache and take what's broken and make it beautiful.

In Jesus' name,
Amen

CHAPTER 8

FOR THE EMPTY NEST MAMA
WHOSE CHILD HAS WALKED
AWAY FROM THEIR FAITH:
PRAYING FOR PRODIGALS

False idols have seduced a generation, and many young adults have been hypnotized by the lies flooding our sin-soaked world. We live in an era where a wicked and unrighteous culture saturates social media and every nook and cranny of society. It is affecting our young people and is far more cunning, evil, and deceptive than we realize, and it is growing worse each year.

While our children were under our roof, we maintained total control. But now, some have gone off the rails because, just like us, they have their own free will. We have given up our control, but as much as we wish He would, God won't force them to follow Him. Believe me, He knows how hard this is, mama. He understands completely, but He is the one in control. He is *never* caught unawares.

Some of you may have children who have chosen a different road and no longer follow the Lord. The path you prepared for them isn't the path they have chosen.

I assumed my daughter would follow in our footsteps of belief, and I'm eternally grateful she did. But there was no formula. In fact, *no* formula guarantees our kids will decide to follow Jesus into adulthood. We can't, but God can. He is still involved whether we see His hand or not. All we can do is teach and model godly principles. But we can never force our children. They must make their own way.

This current culture has bewitched countless young people, goading them onto lanes of distrust, disobedience, and a disregard for the truth they grew up with. Many abandon their faith when they leave home, causing us grief and heartache. God forms their character, and we do our best to instill it, but the Holy Spirit is the only One who can form it in them. Our job is to plant seeds and allow the Holy Spirit to water them. He is the *author and finisher of our faith* (Hebrews 12:2).

We would love nothing more than to see their character fully formed when they leave home. But how can we force them to imitate us? Were any of *our* characters fully formed when we left our parents' nests? Can you look back and see yourself at their age? All of us are growing in maturity as we follow Jesus wholeheartedly. Thank goodness His ways and timelines are not ours!

Loving our prodigal children can be a long and lonely road. Who might contact us next, the police or the hospital? We live with fear, shame, anger, and self-blame. But the empty nest moms of prodigals I know tell me they have one remedy for their children who have walked away: intercession.

The only solution I can wrap my head around is prayer. Prayer for prodigals is powerful. Though *your* heart may be hurting now, trust the Lord with your *child's* heart. The Father is the only one who knows the way they take. Ask the Lord to shine His light into your child's life. Ask Him to send ambassadors of His truth into their lives. What looks alluring to them today may seem empty and cheap tomorrow as God's light shines on it. But in the meantime, let God entice you into your next phase, knowing your children are in His mighty hands.

When I left home, it was a different world. Social media didn't yet exist, and there were no computers or Internet. We had no access to twenty-four hours of daily distraction or constant exposure to the culture like young people have today. We were not sucked in by the siren song of lies about *my* truth, leaving behind *the* truth. Life was not a constant diversion with our heads pointing down, as we pay more attention to our phones than to the lives and loved ones surrounding us.

None of us are fully aware of what we are missing as our eyes are fixed firmly on our phones. We incessantly scroll social media, more absorbed with someone else's life than those standing right in front of us.

The endorphins created by social media are real. Every time we see a like or a new follow, we get an endorphin hit and a false sense of self-worth, ignoring the fact that Jesus *already* counts us worthy if we have trusted Him with our lives. The older I get, the more I realize that Jesus' opinion and approval of me is the *only* one that matters.

We strive to get attention and comments, making the opinions of strangers far more valuable than God's. As much as we wish it were not true, the current culture entices us and our children with every temptation imaginable, doing all it can to bump us off the path of righteousness and boldly pursuing Christ, living for Him and Him alone.

Bonnie

My empty nest got messed up with a son who got addicted to heroin and so much pain for our family... he's alive, and he's now on methadone and lives in our basement at 36 years old... my prayer is for healing and wholeness, and redemption in Jesus's name.

If you are the parent of a prodigal, rest assured that Jesus's work does not end until He returns. Don't give up. God formed their character before they were born, but the Holy Spirit forms it *in* them.

In the parable of the Prodigal Son, Luke 15:11-32, the father knew he couldn't change his son's direction or decision to leave home. All he could do was wait and pray. The son eventually "came to himself," *but not until he came to the end of himself.*

As moms, we plant seeds and water them. We pray and are present for our children. We can intercede for them, petitioning God that whatever tempts them away from His calling for their lives will diminish. Pray that the idols will be exposed, and your children will desire to turn from them. Be available for them as best you can. Ask the Lord to soften their hearts and cause them to hunger for the truth they grew up with.

God doesn't give up on prodigals. – Kate

He is our lighthouse in the storm, leading us home. We raise our kids in the knowledge of Christ and show them His incredible love, but we can never force them to follow. He knows the way that they take...and His timing is always perfect.

One suggestion: if you have a prodigal child, take a few minutes to read Luke 15:11-32, the story of the Prodigal Son. It beautifully illustrates God's profound love and care for your child. And as you read, pray specifically for your child by name, trusting that they will repent and return to the truth. Jesus loves your child even more than you do. Always remember, *Jesus leaves the ninety-nine to seek the one.*

Discussion Questions:

1. If you are the parent of a prodigal, how are you praying for them?
2. Are you able to place them fully in the Lord's hands? If not, why not?
3. How can you trust God with their future?

Scriptures:

- *Bring My sons from afar, and My daughters from the ends of the earth—everyone who is called by My name, whom I have created for My glory. I have formed him, yes, I have made him.* Isaiah 43:6-7
- *What do you think? If a man has a hundred sheep, and one of them goes astray, does he not leave the ninety-nine and go to the mountains to seek the one that is straying? And if he should find it, assuredly, I say to you, he rejoices more over that sheep than over the*

ninety-nine that did not go astray. Even so it is not the will of your Father who is in heaven that one of these little ones should perish. Matthew 18:12-14

- *I will give them a heart to know me, that I am the* LORD. *They will be my people, and I will be their God, for they will return to me with all their heart.* Jeremiah 24:7 (NIV)

- *For thus says the Lord GOD: Behold, I, I myself will search for my sheep and will seek them out. As a shepherd seeks out his flock when he is among his sheep that have been scattered, so will I seek out my sheep, and I will rescue them from all places where they have been scattered on a day of clouds and thick darkness.* Ezekiel 34:11-12 (ESV)

- *When he came to his senses, he said, "How many of my father's hired servants have food to spare, and here I am starving to death! I will set out and go back to my father and say to him: Father, I have sinned against heaven and against you. I am no longer worthy to be called your son; make me like one of your hired servants." So he got up and went to his father.* Luke 15:17-20 (NIV)

A *Prayer* for Moms of Prodigals

Father, You know how heavy my heart is as I've watched my children walk away from the faith they grew up with. But You are the God of redemption and restoration, and You love every one of Your lost sheep.

I lift my child up to You, Lord, I put them in your hands. You know the way that they take. I ask You to pursue them with a love so relentless that they can't deny it. You love them more than I do, and You alone can turn their hearts back to You. Help me release all my mama fears and anxiety to You.

I know You are constantly working behind the scenes, orchestrating circumstances for the good of those who love You. Nothing is impossible for You, and You do immeasurably more than I can *ever* ask or think.

Give me the wisdom I need to understand how best to love and support my child, even from a distance. Remind me to extend grace, forgiveness, understanding, and love, just as you have extended it to me.

All I can do is surrender my children into Your hands, trusting Your faithfulness to protect them and complete the good work You began in them years ago. Holy Spirit, convict them, transform their heart, and draw them back to Your unfailing love. I trust You to mend all that has been broken and to restore all the enemy has stolen.

In Jesus' name,
Amen

CHAPTER 9

A Premature Empty Nest ... and a Beautiful Trust

The book of 1 Samuel holds the remarkable story of a woman who made the bold choice to empty her nest early in her motherhood journey. It is the tender and touching story of Hannah, a devout yet barren woman desperate for a son.

The Bible reveals that Hannah was the first wife of Elkanah, living during the time of the Judges. Though his favored first wife, she was unable to conceive. In 1 Samuel 1:5 we read that *the Lord had closed her womb.* Her rival, Peninah, wife number two, popped out babies year after year, relentlessly provoking Hannah, causing her to grieve and weep bitterly. What did Hannah do? She took her complaint to God. She headed straight to the temple and, in both silence and agonizing sorrow, poured out her petition to the Lord. Eli, the priest, encouraged her that her petition had been heard.

Comforted and strengthened by Eli's words, Hannah headed back to her husband, who was feasting in the house of the Lord. She had spilled out her anguished vow and heartfelt petition to God, convinced He had heard her prayers. Because of her incredible confidence in God's promises, her outlook on life reversed direction *before* her circumstances did. I urge you to read the inspiring (and beautiful) story in 1 Samuel 1:7-20.

Pain was her catalyst for praying an anguished, bold, and life-changing prayer and God heard every word. In desperation, she made the choice to believe the Lord, even in her barrenness. She unselfishly vowed that if the Lord would give her a son, she would return him to His care all the days of his life.

Barrenness always has a purpose. – Kate

Over the course of time, Hannah *did* give birth to a son, naming him Samuel. Her precious time with her baby boy, the joy, laughter, and beautiful chaos every child brings, brought her comfort. But the pending days of honoring her vow hovered over her heart.

Before she knew it, her few years with little Samuel abruptly ended. At three or four years old, after she'd weaned him, Hannah returned to the temple with a sacrifice to fulfill her promise to Eli. With stunning trust and courage, she placed her little boy into his hands, reminding Eli she was the distraught woman he had prayed for in the temple several years before.

Determined to obey the promise she had given the Lord, Hannah selflessly handed over her son when she had no other children at home to fill her table or mend the hole in her heart. She had no guarantee she would *ever* have another child. Her empty nest arrived far earlier than most of ours. Can you imagine her heartache as she faced endless tearful days and lonely nights?

With massive self-sacrifice, Hannah emptied her arms, giving back to God the very gift He had given to her.

I can only wonder what emotions crashed over her as she returned to her quiet and forlorn home with empty arms and a broken heart.

The best antidote to discouragement is to tell God how you truly feel, leaving the outcome to Him. – Kate

Once each year, Hannah traveled to the temple with her offering, bringing Samuel a little robe she made for him. What joy and longing must have swirled in her heart. She could see him and give him his little robe ... yet because of her vow, she had to turn her back and walk away, leaving him behind.

As hard as it might be to watch our adult children leave the nest, try to imagine the hurt and heartache Hannah suffered each time she walked away. She had one choice as we do: trust that the Lord would protect and keep her little boy. Oh, the tears she must have cried!

After a few years, and because of her awe-inspiring obedience, the Lord allowed her empty nest to be filled to overflowing with five more children. Because of her faithfulness, *And the Lord visited Hannah, so that she conceived and bore three sons and two daughters. Meanwhile the child Samuel grew before the Lord.* 1 Samuel 2:21

Samuel grew up to be the greatest priest and prophet in the Bible. But Hannah, like Moses' mother Jochebed, had to let him go. She trusted the Lord's plan, leaving his future in God's hands.

We, too, are asked to obey and give our children back to God. He urges us to give them over to Him, *trusting their lives to his care.* Hannah's life is proof that, for many of us, our heavy and sacrificial obedience can beget a beautiful blessing.

Discussion Questions:

1. What conflicting emotions have you experienced since your child left the nest?
2. How have you begun to see His blessing in your obedience as you have let them go?
3. What are some ways you are learning to trust the Lord in this new season?

Scriptures:

- *Fear not, for I am with you. Be not dismayed, for I am your God. I will strengthen you, Yes, I will help you. I will uphold you with My righteous right hand.* Isaiah 41:10
- *And we know that all things work together for good to those who love God, to those who are the called according to His purpose.* Romans 8:28
- *The Lord is my strength and my shield. My heart trusted in Him, and I am helped. Therefore my heart greatly rejoices, and with my song I will praise Him.* Psalm 28:7

A Prayer For Release

Father, You have blessed me with the gift of motherhood, and I am eternally grateful. You are the God who sees my tears and hears my cry. You have heard every prayer I've prayed throughout the seasons of raising my children. You answered Hannah's prayer for a child and gave her the joy of motherhood, and You answered mine. I am deeply humbled by Your grace and mercy to me.

I ask that you guide, protect, and draw my children closer to you. May they walk in Your ways and live lives that bring honor and glory to Your holy name.

Give me the strength to embrace new opportunities, possibilities, challenges, and changes as I enter my empty nest. While I cherish all the memories of the years with my children, help me find joy in this present moment, as I look forward to a new season with excitement and enthusiasm.

Send Your Comforter, the Holy Spirit, when loneliness or sadness threatens to engulf me, reminding me to lean on You and You alone for strength and solace. I trust in Your unfailing love because I know You continually guide and sustain me.

Like Hannah, I rejoice in Your salvation and Your great faithfulness. You alone are my rock and my redeemer, and I will praise You all the days of my life.

In Jesus' name,
Amen

THE WORK

CHAPTER 10

EMPTY NEST MOMS AND THE POWER OF PRAYER

After navigating the empty nest for nearly two decades, I am convinced that prayer is our ultimate and most powerful weapon. Hopefully, my experience will help prepare you for your After Party.

Prayer is *the* most necessary ingredient for apprehending God's will for our lives. Nothing can quiet the chaos in our minds quite like spending time in His word and worshipping in His presence.

Prayer has a massive impact, bearing more fruit than we can begin to imagine, and it is worth any and every investment of time.

God created the world with four words: *Then God said, "Let there be light"; and there was light.* (Genesis 1:3, emphasis added). Four simple words and an entire universe blazed into being. We can't begin to process the true power of the spoken word. When we pray, circumstances can change, even if they are blocked from our sight. Jesus is the Word made flesh, and every one of His miracles illustrates the incredible power of words.

So Jesus answered and said to him, "What do you want Me to do for you?" The blind man said to Him, "Rabboni, that I may receive my sight." Then Jesus said to him, "Go your way;

your faith has made you well." And immediately he received his sight and followed Jesus on the road. Mark 10:51-52

When Satan tempted Jesus during His forty days in the wilderness, Jesus rebuked him soundly three times with scripture, saying, *It is written...* Both Satan and Jesus knew the indescribable and creative power in God's word.

God hears every one of our prayers, whether spoken or prayed silently. My personal preference is to pray out loud, especially scripture. *So then faith comes by hearing, and hearing by the word of God* (Romans 10:17). When praying out loud, our faith can be significantly reinforced as we hear our words.

Praying His word is simply agreeing with God as we speak His words back to Him. When you are unsure what to pray, ask the Holy Spirit to show you. Scripture reminds us that *we have the mind of Christ* (1 Corinthians 2:16). Because we *do* have His mind, we can trust that Jesus will share His thoughts with us.

When praying for ourselves or others, we can insert our name or theirs right in the scripture. This can help us personalize our prayers, reminding us that God is a personal God, and *He knows our names.*

Honestly, if we could handle everything life throws at us in our own strength, why would we need to pray? He alone is the God of the impossible. Without Him, I can do nothing, but with Him, I can do all things!

If you already have an idea of what your next steps might be, ask the Lord to confirm His word to you so you don't waste precious time doing something He hasn't ordained for you to do. Dream and pray big, audacious prayers. The Bible says *you do not have because you do not ask* (James 4:2). Be an asker!

Through life experiences and stepping out in my own strength way too often, the Holy Spirit has demonstrated the manifest truth of this scripture: *Let us therefore come boldly to the throne of grace, that we may obtain mercy and find grace to help in time of need* (Hebrews 4:16).

Persist in Prayer

Who wouldn't want their lives to produce lasting fruit? Who wouldn't want to be strong and effective in our next season? If the Lord is showing you something about your future, be bold and ask Him for audacious faith! Believe the truth of what the Lord is showing you as you move into your After Party.

> *Persist in prayer with a heart open to God's whispers. His will for your life is not a secret but a revelation waiting to be discovered in His perfect timing.* – Kate

Consistency is Key. I love the way the Amplified Bible, Classic Edition, translates Matthew 7:7-8.

> *Keep on asking and it will be given you; keep on seeking and you will find; keep on knocking [reverently] and [the door] will be opened to you. For everyone who keeps on asking receives; and he who keeps on seeking finds; and to him who keeps on knocking, [the door] will be opened.*

Discussion Questions:

1. How do you think you might be bolder in prayer?
2. What is God showing you about your future?

3. What changes do you need to make so you can persist in your prayer life?

Scriptures:

- *In the day when I cried out, You answered me, And made me bold with strength in my soul.* Psalm 138:3
- *... in whom we have boldness and access with confidence through faith in Him.* Ephesians 3:12
- *Let us therefore come boldly to the throne of grace, that we may obtain mercy and find grace to help in time of need.* Hebrews 4:16
- *So then faith comes by hearing, and hearing by the word of God.* Romans 10:17

Prayer for Wisdom in Praying

Lord, as I begin to seek Your will for this phase of my life, give me wisdom to discern Your voice. This world is noisy and confusing, easily distracting me from what is important.

Show me truth as I read Your word because I know Your word is the only word I will ever need. Help me persist in prayer, not tempted to give up when my prayers aren't answered the way I'd hoped. As I read the Bible, show me how to apply it to my life, because I know Your word *is* life.

I can't figure all this out on my own, but I am confident You have all the answers I seek.

Prayer has great impact. I know You hear every prayer I pray and that faith comes by hearing Your word. Give me the boldness I need to move into the next phase of my life. Whatever comes or whatever plans You may have for me, *I will trust You.*

In Jesus' name,

Amen

CHAPTER 11

GOD IS IN THE DETAILS

If you don't get the answer to your prayer at first, pray again! We can pray both short-term and long-term prayers. God instructs us to ask, seek, knock, and prevail in prayer. You may pray some prayers for decades, including prayers for specific healings, salvation of family members, open doors for ministry, etc.

The earnest (heartfelt, continued) prayer of a righteous man makes tremendous power available [dynamic in its working]. (James 5:16 AMPCE)

We need to be continuous and consistent in prayer. Why? Because God tells us to.

I have made a holy habit of writing down my prayers in a pretty journal, the ones I pray regularly, and adding new prayers as needs arise. Looking back and reflecting on all the answered prayers, it becomes abundantly clear that our lives matter greatly to God. He cares about all our pains, struggles, hopes, and heartaches.

As the new year begins, I write down my long-term prayers. If a prayer from last year hasn't been answered yet, it stays on the list. I like to add dates and note how God chose to answer. Don't stop praying unless God reveals that you are praying in error.

❧

Malinda

My one and only son chose to go to school 1200 miles away. I was nervous leaving my son but excited for him at the same time. So many emotions. I cried the entire way to the airport, the entire flight home, and for the next week while lying on his bed.

My husband decided to file for divorce, which I didn't see coming. I would be completely alone. Piled on top of that, my dad suddenly died from a massive heart attack.

I dug deep and prayed like I had never prayed before. I knew I didn't have time to feel sorry for myself. I needed to show my son that I was okay.

So, God's way to show me how to be an empty nester was a hard road, but I found that I needed to live my best life and find the things that made me truly happy. So, my advice to anyone headed to an empty nest is to think about who you are and what things make you happy and go live it. You and your kids will all be better for it.

❧

Please do not give up! God's timing is everything. If He has closed one door, ask Him to open another. You may well be praying for a *good* thing, but God has the *best* thing in mind for you. The longer I've walked with the Lord, He has consistently shown me that good is the enemy of the best every time. (Remember, God specifically told Adam and Eve not to eat from the tree of *good* and evil.)

Eating the good will satisfy us. Waiting
for God's best will purify us. – Kate

No detail is too trivial to annoy God, and no idea is too ridiculous to put Him off or scare Him away. God has challenged my faith over the years by prompting me to pray for the big and the impossible, and He has answered those big, impossible prayers time after time. His answers don't always show up as I hoped or expected, but they *always* show up.

What if you got together with a group of empty nester friends and had an After Party prayer party? Begin praying for each other as you seek God for your next season. Agree together with your group as you commit issues to prayer. It will strengthen friendships and provide much-needed accountability during this season.

Pray together for each other's children. Coming into agreement with others is an amazing opportunity for fellowship and possibly life-changing answers to your prayers. God will often reveal things to others that you may have overlooked or cannot see.

Time on our knees is the most profitable
time we will ever spend. – Kate

Have you read Psalm 139 recently? It is one of my all-time favorite psalms. I love everything about it because it proves *God thought us up as He created us.* He saw us before we were ever in our mother's wombs and prearranged *every single day* of our lives. Here's my favorite section:

For You formed my inward parts; You covered me in
my mother's womb. I will praise You, for I am fearfully
and wonderfully made. Marvelous are Your works,

and that my soul knows very well. My frame was not hidden from You, when I was made in secret, and skillfully wrought in the lowest parts of the earth. Your eyes saw my substance, being yet unformed. And in Your book they all were written, the days fashioned for me, when as yet there were none of them.

How precious also are Your thoughts to me, O God! How great is the sum of them! If I should count them, they would be more in number than the sand. When I awake, I am still with You. Psalm 139:13-18

It stuns me to realize that God's thoughts towards us are more than the grains of sand or the stars in the sky. Does it boggle your mind as it does mine that He has counted every single hair on our heads? He loves us *that much!*

He is in the details! And because of that, we can pray detailed prayers–sometimes *very* detailed prayers for our family.

In my journal, each family member has a page or two. As prayers are answered, they are checked off, and new ones are added when needed. Prayers for general things like safe travel, energy, good health, devotion to the Lord, and much more. He prompts me to pray in detail for whatever needs deeper prayer. You get the idea. Because nothing is too small to pray about, even good parking spots.

Most of the time, I get good parking spots, but not every time. *But you don't get what you don't ask for.*

When our daughter moved out on her own to Nashville, we began praying specifically for every detail of her life as it moved full speed ahead, petitioning God for everything you can imagine, and inviting a group of close friends to pray with us.

We prayed for good health, wise choices, and discernment in all her decisions. A lot of significant opportunities were on the horizon, so we recognized the importance of praying pre-emptively. We couldn't be with her every minute and didn't know what her day-to-day schedule looked like. Because we were in Florida and she was in Nashville, we were deeply impressed to pray consistent and detailed prayers. Nothing was too small. And no detail is ever too small for any mom to pray for her children.

So let me encourage you. Don't shy away from praying audacious, impossible, detailed, big *(and small)*, bold prayers. God is a big God. He can handle it. You can be sure that if you are praying outside His will, He will show you.

Discussion Questions:

1. Do you prevail in prayer, or do you give up too soon? Why do you think that is?
2. What God dreams do you have for this next season?
3. How will you pray for your dream, even when it seems impossible?
4. List a few answers to prayer that you have experienced in your family.
5. How can you make your prayers more detailed and specific?
6. What kind of long-term prayers are you praying?

Scriptures:

- *Now faith is the substance of things hoped for, the evidence of things not seen.* Hebrews 11:1
- *O Lord, You have searched me and known me. You know my sitting down and my rising up. You understand my thought afar off. You comprehend my path and my lying down, and are acquainted with all my ways. For there is not a word on my tongue, but behold, O Lord, You know it altogether.* Psalm 139:1-4
- *Death and life are in the power of the tongue, and those who love it will eat its fruit.* Proverbs 18:21
- *The earnest (heartfelt, continued) prayer of a righteous man makes tremendous power available [dynamic in its working].* James 5:16 (AMPCE)
- *But the very hairs of your head are all numbered. Do not fear therefore; you are of more value than many sparrows.* Luke 12:7

A Prayer of Belief

Father, I know prayer is the most powerful force in the universe and I recognize what a privilege it is to pray. In Your word, You invite us to come boldly before the throne of grace to ask for help in times of need. So, with humility, I approach Your throne knowing that You hear and answer every prayer I pray.

Your word promises in Philippians 4:6-7 that when we pray according to Your will You will grant us peace. Teach me to trust in Your timing and plan, knowing that Your ways and thoughts are higher than mine.

Give me faith that moves mountains. I know absolutely nothing is impossible for You, and I know You do immeasurably more than we could ever ask or think. Prompt me to pray fervently and persistently, making prayer a daily priority. I know power is released when we pray.

Give me the courage to pray with boldness and to prevail in prayer until You answer. Show me that nothing is too small or too big to pray about. Remind me that faith is the substance of things hoped for, the evidence of things not seen. Inspire me to continue in prayer even when my prayer seems impossible. Embolden me to *be an asker.*

May my prayers for others be a source of blessing and encouragement.

Thank You for giving me the weighty and formidable privilege of prayer, knowing You are always listening. I am determined to make prayer the cornerstone of my life as it anchors me in Your presence and guides me in Your will.

In Jesus' name,
Amen

CHAPTER 12

THE EMPTY NEST IS THE PERFECT SEASON TO DREAM WITH THE FATHER

Has God dropped a crazy dream in your heart? What out-of-the-box adventure is He inviting you to join? For most empty nest moms, the tried-and-true escape clause of *not having the time to undertake anything new* is not what it once was. The kids are gone. The nest is empty, and the *what do I do now* blank canvas is waiting for you and God to fill in.

Is He asking you to do something you know you cannot do on your own, like He asked Gideon, Esther, Moses, Ruth, and dozens of other Bible heroes? Has God invited you to undertake something so impossible that you won't even attempt it because you are afraid you might fall flat on your face?

Because of how the Father has prompted me to believe the impossible, I have learned that God often challenges us to do more and go farther than we ever thought possible.

Dreaming with the Father requires us to believe, obey, and take Him at His word. Does God say what He means and means what He says?

As we persevere, we will eventually get out of our own heads and into God's purposes. For some of us, He'll ask if we will say yes to something arduous and demanding. God searches for the ones willing to change the world, willing to obey and say yes, even if the yes costs everything. We cannot imagine how weighty His dreams are for us … and how profound His purpose for our lives.

Because our nest is empty, many of us now have the time and bandwidth to return to what we may have laid down or put aside during the years we were raising our children. Saying yes takes absolute trust during our After Party.

Maybe you are ready to take on the next adventure with all the power you have or think you have, but as reality presses in, you admit you are plum worn out. Over it. Dog tired of trying to work life out in your own strength and in your own power. I get it. You are weary of trying to be all the things for all the people in your life. But the harder we try, the more powerless we find our power to be. Our only hope is depending on Jesus, exchanging our burdens for His.

Nancy

I put on my brave face as I kissed my daughter goodbye at the airport.

Who am I now, Lord? I've been homeschooling for two decades. What am I to do now? I have no purpose! My nest was empty, and my heart and soul felt empty, too.

Over the following year, I prayed for direction. God began to nudge me toward a childhood dream of being a nurse. At age 48, could I take on such a daunting endeavor?

So, I took the plunge. Two years later, at age 50, I began my career as an RN. Those two years represent one of the hardest things I've ever done (besides raising children!). And one of the most rewarding.

Taking care of patients filled my need to nurture them. Serving as a missionary nurse in Haiti and Africa gave me purpose. Doing such a hard thing in mid-life proved God's faithfulness to me, preparing me for the next milestone that unfolded after I retired in 2018.

Have you ever wondered, *"What if?"* What if you actually wrote that book, started that business, or charted a course to a new career as Nancy did? What if God called you to missions or ministry? Would you go? What if you went back to school to get or add to your degree? What if you had the opportunity to volunteer at the single mom's ministry or homeless shelter?

It is not too late. You are only limited by your imagination. God will begin to arouse what may have lain dormant for decades. Has He dropped a crazy double-dog-dare idea into your spirit? Pray and ask for confirmation. Seek advice and get counsel from trusted and mature women. Ask them to pray with you to gain discernment for what He is calling you to do. And then do it.

*As we begin to step into and embrace our
next season, we may find fear turning to
courage, courage to faith, and our nagging
doubts transformed into trust.* – Kate

We may not feel equipped to jump into what He is
offering us right away. Why? Because He is inviting us
into the unknown ... and if you are anything like me,
you may not feel remotely equipped *at all*. But that's
okay.

Stepping Off the Ledge

When we have no idea what God has in store for us,
it can be ever so hard to trust Him with our futures.
However, He knows our capabilities and our weak-
nesses far better than we do, and He is the ultimate
judge of the tools we need to accomplish the task He
has assigned to us.

As we walk into His purposes for our lives and
our families, our faith and trust will strengthen
into a resolve to take God's word to heart and, with
boldness, parachute into the life He is inviting us to
live.

Mama, if fear is holding you back, let me ask you
this question: Where is your strength and determina-
tion rooted? Where is your bravery? Will you face the
fears that hound you?

This is the season to rebut the lies you have been
told and the lies you may have told yourself. It's time to
defeat rejection and rise above low self-esteem and the
spirit of worthlessness that may have shadowed you (as
they shadowed me) since you were a child.

It's time to gather up your courage and step into the new enterprise God has ordained for you. *Don't let fear own you anymore.*

Who told you that you don't have what it takes? Who tried to convince you you're not smart enough or young enough? Who told you God has nothing for you and can't use you?

> *It's time to unsubscribe from lies the world*
> *continues to throw at us.* – Kate

He is seeking our yes, even when our yes makes no sense—*especially* if it makes no sense. Those of us willing to step off the ledge and catapult into our future can rest assured He will be there to catch us and equip us and not allow us to crash into the gaping, cavernous pit below. He's got you.

Know this: the water gets deeper as you go out. It's a matter of complete trust.

As so many biblical heroes and heroines prove, God provides divine opportunities for us to choose to be used by Him to accomplish His holy purposes. But, in His wisdom, He has given us free will. We can cave to fear and say no if we choose, and sadly, most do. But we are not among the *most* when we decide once and for all to wholeheartedly trust and step out in faith.

World-changers like Hannah, Mary, Esther, and Ruth had no idea they were altering history. But because they were willing to risk everything, face their fears, and obey God, they marched resolutely into their destinies, changed the world, and God honored their faith.

Sure, we can choose to listen to all the lying voices crying out their false platitudes:

"You are in control of your life."
"You are the hero of your story."
"God failed you."
"You can do it yourself."
"She needed a hero, so she became one."

These voices strive desperately to convince us we alone control our future. But we do not. As Isaiah 46:10 (RSV) reminds us, God says, *My counsel shall stand, and I will accomplish all my purpose.*

❧

Michelle

I'd always wanted to be a writer. When our youngest turned ten, I attended a writer's conference. After a dreary day with little encouragement, I watched it rain and told God, "I might just as well go home and raise our daughter. It will be a bummer if I'm never published, but worse if I ruin raising her."

Right then, the rain stopped, the clouds parted, and a sunbeam shone down. I laughed. "I'll take that as a promise."

When she left for college, my 30 years of in-house parenting ended. We'd seen it coming, of course, and were prepared. We dropped her off at college, drove to the airport, and took a long weekend/business trip to Washington, D.C. It was just the two of us.

But something else happened that momentous day.

As we drove to the college in our loaded car, I got a phone call from my literary agent. She'd sold my first writing project, and I received a contract that very day. My long-desired writing career began the day my parenting career (sort of) ended.

Since then, the time I devoted to parenting (and carpooling!) switched to writing. Dreams, family, and God take us to interesting places. Embracing them and then letting go has always worked best for me.

Swallow moms are more apt to jump off the ledge into the new adventure God is calling them to. Robin moms take a bit more time to make the leap, but eventually they will take the risk after weighing all their options. Melancholy Mourning Dove moms, like I was during that season, are more apt to argue with God, telling Him all the reasons they can't possibly do what He is calling them to do.

There is a God-sized dream with your name on it, waiting to be unwrapped. If you grab hold of it, trusting His wisdom about the future He has ordained for you, the pieces will assemble, they'll fall into place, and you will find the answers you seek.

I see it as a *spiritual bungee jump* because that is exactly what it feels like. We jump, risking our future, our agenda, and our comfort to step into the divine destination God has for us—and pray the bungee cord holds, and we don't crash onto the rocks below!

The good news is that God's bungee cords *never* fail. You will see crazy change if you're willing to tap into His crazy idea.

Trust in the wait, for God's timing is perfect.
Your God-sized dream is woven with threads
of divine purpose and destiny. – Kate

Jesus has challenged me more than once that even my mustard seed-sized faith is sufficient for me to step out and trust God with my life. We all have *at least* the faith of a mustard seed! But many of us have trouble trusting that tiny seed of faith.

Many who hear God's dare will not take the risk. Those of us who have walked with Jesus through life's challenges are quite aware that our faith gets tested and tossed around regularly. And unless we allow situations forcing us to believe and stretch and grow, we cannot ever truly know that God is with us wherever He calls us.

Your season *will* arrive. You may be in the middle of it as you read this book. If not, rest assured that in the fullness of time, and when it serves God's purposes, the day will come when you walk into the heartbeat of His divine plan for your After Party, stepping squarely into your future.

Don't Miss Your Moment

Have you heard the fascinating story of Reinhard Bonnke, a distinguished evangelist and founder of Christ For The Nations, who spent much of his ministry in Africa? Because of his obedience to God's calling, tens of millions of souls came into the kingdom. In fact, he is considered the Billy Graham of Africa. But here is what's most fascinating about Bonnke: He was not God's first choice.

One day, God made it crystal clear to Bonnke that before He asked him to take on this daunting ministry, He had invited *(dared)* two other men to shoulder this huge task for Him. Both turned Him down. Can you imagine? Maybe it was fear that stopped them, maybe complacency, or a lack of willingness to shoulder a new task or to sacrifice their comfortable lives. Maybe they judged the price as simply too high.

There *is* a price attached to following Jesus. Nowhere in His word does He promise that following Him will be easy. In fact, He is adamant that it is a narrow road few find.

Can you imagine what those two men discovered when they made it to heaven and Jesus showed them the life He had planned and called them to... the life they *could* have had? How must they have felt when they realized they had missed the divine plan for their lives, and He'd given their rejected assignment to another?

In heaven, when God displayed the fruit that was born from Bonnke's "yes," the souls that were saved, and the assignment that had been written in the books of their lives, what went through their minds? They had turned down the Creator of the Universe. Honestly, that terrifies me.

The truth is, we can say no to God if we want to. His assignments often appear daunting and impossible to accomplish. But He will only ask us to do what He knows we *can* do.

Are you willing to dream with God? Will you go wherever He leads? Are you ready to count the cost? Will you choose to be chosen to change the world? I hope so. We need you in the body of Christ. We need your life, your voice, your compassion, your gifts, and your talents... we need YOU.

Discussion Questions:

1. What if you actually took God at His word? What would change in your life?

2. What's stopping you from moving into your After Party with faith and expectation?
3. Will you step outside your safe haven and into God's next season? What might that look like?
4. Are you convinced you can change the world? How? If not, why not?
5. What is God daring you to do?

Scriptures:

- *"For I know the plans I have for you," declares the L*ORD, *"plans to prosper you and not to harm you, plans to give you hope and a future."* Jeremiah 29:11 (NIV)
- *... and he went out, not knowing whither he went.* Hebrews 11:8 (KJV)
- *... So also Abraham "believed God, and it was credited to him as righteousness."* Galatians 3:6 NIV
- *My brethren, count it all joy when you fall into various trials, knowing that the testing of your faith produces patience.* James 1:2-3

A Prayer for Boldness

Father, even though my children have moved on, I know my purpose in this life is not over. I'm standing on the threshold of a brand-new season, and I need Your guidance to step into the calling and direction You have ordained for me.

You have plans for me, good plans to prosper and not harm me, to give me hope and a future. Teach me to trust in all Your promises and grant me the ability to embrace the unique calling You have placed on my life.

I need Your boldness to follow and trust Your plan with courage and confidence, knowing that if You have called me to it, You will equip me to do it.

As You fill me with Your Holy Spirit, give me fearlessness to follow, willing to take risks for Your kingdom. Keep fear far from me and fill me with an intrepid spirit.

Help me overcome the insecurities trying to hold me back from obeying You and walking fully into my calling.

I surrender all my plans, hopes, and dreams to You. Your ways and thoughts are far higher than mine and I only want Your will done in my life. Thank You for the privilege of being Your servant and for the opportunity to make an impact in Your kingdom. Allow me to see the possibilities You've placed in front of me, with a heart eager to respond with both love and obedience.

In Jesus' name,
Amen

CHAPTER 13

THE DESTINY OF THE DILIGENT: SEVEN WAYS TO PREPARE NOW FOR THEN

For those of you with children still home, what can you begin doing *now* to prepare for *then?* How can you efficiently use what I call *working in the margins,* those moments when you have extra time on your hands? They are the chunks of time between all your mothering tasks when you have a bit of breathing room, moments you can begin to think about the future when the kiddos are out of the house.

Beginning to work on your goals now will help soften the pain of the empty nest... you will have something exciting and concrete to look forward to when your last child leaves.

My best advice? Prepare and practice *now.*

For to everyone who has, more will be given, and he will have abundance; but from him who does not have, even what he has will be taken away (Matthew 25:29).

You might feel called to start your own business. Maybe you've been dreaming about it for years, but God has made it clear this is not the right time. There is a perfect moment because God is the Lord of seasons and timing. So, what should you do while you wait?

Study all you can about small businesses. Meet small business owners and ask if they will mentor you. Take online classes or tutorials. If you are able, work part-time in a small local business to gain experience. Learn the rules and regulations in your area, etc. Work on your skills. Do something to prepare for your future.

How do you find those "margins?" Think about what you are doing when you're waiting in the carpool line or sitting at the doctor's office or at your child's dance or baseball practice.

Can you get out of bed thirty or sixty minutes early and spend quiet time with the Lord? He may well give you ideas that have never entered your mind.

What about turning off the TV and closing your phone? Scrolling through social media or watching Netflix are delightful diversions but they can never move you forward to achieving your goals. A steady diet of distraction will make for a malnourished spirit and wastes precious time.

Maybe God has called you to missions or ministry. Are there a few extra hours a week to volunteer at your church or the local outreach you hope to serve when your empty nest years arrive? And can your children accompany you? Does God want to raise you up in politics, and you can feel it in your bones? What candidate can you begin to volunteer for now? Do you want to finish your degree? What online classes you can take in the meantime?

There are as many paths as there are people. You will soon find you have more time than you realize to start climbing a new and exciting learning curve. Don't let the size or scope of your vision overwhelm you ... *you only need to do the next right thing.* It's fine to dream big but keep your focus small for now. Take a step that moves the ball toward your goal.

What modest step can you make to propel yourself forward? Remember, somebody needs what you have and what you've been ordained to do.

These ideas might help:

- *Start small.* Work on one aspect of one skill rather than trying to learn all the details. You don't have to master every last step all at once. Take one bite at a time.
- *Set Goals.* A dream without a goal is merely a dream. Set realistic and attainable goals. Examine what you want to achieve and set practical goals for what you can accomplish in those margins where you have daily moments to spare. You'll find more info about this in the chapter on goal setting.
- *Utilize technology.* There are lots of online resources to discover and use. You can find tutorials, podcasts, downloads, classes, and videos— all of which can help you develop the skills you need at your own pace.
- *Find a mentor.* Do you know someone who is an expert in the field you feel called to? Ask them for guidance and advice. Offer to volunteer for them. Sit under their tutelage and learn from them.
- *Join or create a community.* Social media outlets offer a wide variety of groups for just about any and every topic you can dream of. Or find an

in-person group or an individual in your area who is pursuing the same goals you are. Share what you're learning to support and keep each other accountable. I'm part of a local writer's group—nothing fancy, but the perfect place for me to share what I'm working on with other writers and a safe place to receive valuable advice and solid critique of my work.

- *Practice.* Regular practice is critical if you are determined to learn a new skill. Make time to practice, even if it's just for a few hours a week.
- *Be patient.* Learning anything new takes time. You see this in your children as they begin to grasp a new skill like reading or algebra. Your adventure does not materialize all at once. Be patient with yourself and don't allow discouragement to take root. If you are consistent, when you look back a year from now, you will be amazed to see how much further you are toward achieving your goal ... further than you ever dreamed was possible! For those of you who don't have a clue what's next, that is perfectly okay. I had no idea what God had in store for me when my empty nest season erupted. It took me completely by surprise, but I was willing to swallow hard, set aside my fear, and do what I knew God had called me to do. You might not know your next step right now, but He will be sure to tell you when the time is right. And it might come as a complete surprise, something that never crossed your mind.

As you follow these tips, you'll find you can set the course and learn a new skill, even when your time is limited. Pat yourself on the back, knowing you are learning and growing.

Discussion Questions:

1. Do you know what God is calling you to do when your children are grown and gone? What is it?
2. How can you begin to prepare *now* for *then?*
3. What goals can you set as you begin?
4. What community can you join or online class can you take to get you ready for your After Party?
5. Where can you begin to find margins in your life?

Scriptures:

- *For to everyone who has, more will be given, and he will have abundance; but from him who does not have, even what he has will be taken away.* Matthew 25:29
- *For who has despised the day of small things?* Zechariah 4:10
- *But you, be strong and do not let your hands be weak, for your work shall be rewarded!* 2 Chronicles 15:7
- *Delight yourself also in the LORD, and He shall give you the desires of your heart. Commit your way to the LORD, trust also in Him, and He shall bring it to pass.* Psalm 37:4-5
- *And He said to me, "My grace is sufficient for you, for My strength is made perfect in weakness." Therefore most gladly I will rather boast in my infirmities, that the power of Christ may rest upon me.* 2 Corinthians 12:9
- *And whatever you do, do it heartily, as to the Lord and not to men, knowing that from the Lord you will receive*

the reward of the inheritance; for you serve the Lord Christ. Colossians 3:23-24

A Prayer for Diligence

Father, Your word reminds us that whatever we do, we are to do it with all our might, working for You, not men. May I begin each new day with strong commitment and tenacity, knowing I am serving You in everything I do.

Help me to discern Your will and to prioritize the tasks and responsibilities You have set before me. May I be trustworthy in all that You have put in my hands.

I will do my best to recognize what my margins are, those bits of time I can use to work on my future.

Distraction and procrastination can woo me away from my calling. Guard my heart against diversions and misdirection that can so easily drag me away from what You have chosen me to do. Teach me to persevere despite setbacks and challenges.

May I be diligent in prayer and the study of Your word, seeking Your guidance every day. I ask for a spirit of excellence in everything I do, big or small, so that my life might always glorify You.

Thank You, Father, for the strength You provide and for reminding me that Your grace is always sufficient for whatever You might call me to do. Your power is made perfect in my weakness. As I lean on You, give me strength and joy in serving You until my last breath.

In Jesus' name,

Amen

CHAPTER 14

An Empty Nest and the Value in Volunteering

Volunteering takes us out of ourselves, our cares, and our worries, allowing us to focus on the needs of others. If it fits into your life right now, you'll find it is chock full of benefits as well as deeply rewarding. If your kids are old enough, ask them to volunteer with you.

There are countless organizations with enormous needs, and they would be thrilled to have your help. When your nest is empty at last, you will have established relationships within organizations that value your help and support.

When I entered my empty nest, I volunteered at a single mom's ministry. I loved my time there for two reasons: I was helping women during a difficult season and making beautiful friendships. Years before that, I volunteered at a crisis pregnancy center, counseling women during a critical and vulnerable time in their lives.

Volunteering lowers our stress levels. It helps release tension, improve mood, and boost contentment and well-being.

Here are a few other benefits:

- *Personal fulfillment.* Volunteering fills us with a deep sense of significance as we recognize how our work impacts many, making a Christ-honoring difference in our communities.
- *Developing new skills.* We have an opportunity to learn brand-new skills while honing existing ones.
- *Career opportunities.* We gain valuable experience and make connections in our field of interest, leading to new opportunities and relationships. For example, if your goal is to go into ministry when you hit the empty nest, volunteer at your church or a ministry center now. Maybe your heart is to start a moms group in your area for a specific need, say parenting teens. Now is the perfect time to begin building the foundation. What is your vision? Look into local and online groups for inspiration and how they are structured, so you'll have a better understanding of the how-to when you have more time.
- *Increased sense of community.* As we positively impact our communities, we will experience a profound sense of satisfaction, happiness, and well-being.
- *Contribution to society.* Volunteering brings positive value to many as we gift our time and effort to the well-being of others.
- *Personal growth.* Volunteering can be challenging, but at the same time, we develop new skills and find immense gratification in knowing we are changing lives.

- *Networking.* Volunteering provides a great opportunity to meet new people, including possible employers or mentors...as well as the added benefit of making new friends.
- *Changing the world.* When we step out of ourselves to help others, we can share the one thing no one else can... *us!*

Discussion Questions:

1. Have you ever volunteered? Where and for whom? What were your takeaways?
2. What kind of volunteering would you like to do?
3. What might be the value in letting your older children volunteer with you?

Scriptures:

- *Our people must learn to devote themselves to doing what is good, in order to provide for urgent needs and not live unproductive lives.* Titus 3:14 (NIV)
- *I have shown you in every way, by laboring like this, that you must support the weak. And remember the words of the Lord Jesus, that He said, 'It is more blessed to give than to receive.'* Acts 20:35
- *Let each of you look out not only for his own interests, but also for the interests of others.* Philippians 2:4
- *Each of you should use whatever gift you have received to serve others, as faithful stewards of God's grace in its various forms.* 1 Peter 4:10 (NIV)

A Prayer for Connection

Father, now that I have more time on my hands, I want to begin serving others. I am well aware of the deep need in my community. Give me discernment to know where You would have me serve and how I can best use my gifts and talents to bless others.

Open my eyes to see the hurts and needs all around me. Fill my heart with compassion to reach out, offering a helping hand to others in practical ways. More than anything I want to bring Your light into the lives of the hurting and the distressed.

Give me the courage to step out and into the role You have for me right here where I live. Let Your strength overcome any doubts or worries that might hold me back, and the boldness to walk in faith, knowing You are equipping me and calling me to a good work.

I pray that I will serve with humility and grace, doing whatever You put in my hand with joy. Let my service touch hearts and use me as an avenue demonstrating Your love and peace, a love that transforms lives. Remind me that it's not about me, it's about how I can honor You with my time and talents.

Thank you for the opportunities You are going to give me and for the fulfillment that following You brings. I thank you Holy Spirit that you are guiding me and giving me exactly what I need as I step out in faith to serve You.

In Jesus' name,
Amen

THE FOCUS

CHAPTER 15

Marriage First … You Are More Than Roommates

Invest in your marriage.

The current culture notwithstanding, if you are married, you and your husband very likely chose each other *before* you had children. As you approach your empty nest, this is the opportune time to work on and strengthen your relationship. If your marriage to date hasn't been as rock solid as it could be, take time to join forces, creating an example of a healthy marriage your kids can emulate one day.

Love carried your children *into* the world and love will equip them to venture *out*.

Purposely make time to go on dates to demonstrate the model of a healthy, romantic marriage. If you have children still at home, take time to be together without them. Make your husband a priority in your life. Remember, he will still be there when the kiddos, and the Legos, and the Cheerios are long gone. Celebrate this next stage!

Do you have something fun you both love to do? Plan a time when you can get away and do whatever you both enjoy and can look forward to.

Before your child was a twinkle in your eye, your husband was there for you. After your last child is long gone, your husband will *still* be there for you. As we raise our families, it is easy to forget, in all the chaos and busyness, that our children are going to grow up, leave home, and be launched into the life God calls them to. If troubles have been brewing under the surface of your marriage, they can begin to bubble up once the children leave home.

> *The empty nest is the perfect stage for couples to write their own love story, chapter two.* – Kate

Childrearing is only a part of our lives. If we make children our *only* priority and ignore the relationship with our spouse, what will happen when the kids leave? Where does that leave our marriage? And what are the predictable consequences of allowing this crucial relationship to wither?

The last thing we want is to become a stranger to our husbands. Dig in now to build and strengthen your relationship. Remember, you are called as a wife *first* and as a mom second.

Have you heard of the phenomenon called Gray Divorce? For couples over fifty, the divorce rate in the US has nearly doubled since 2004 and has *more* than doubled for couples over sixty-five. Why? Loneliness, focusing on our own happiness, different opinions on finances, and diverse interests have all contributed.

Another factor is how the two handle an empty nest. Do couples still have shared or complementary goals, or have they drifted apart?

It can be dangerous to take any of this for granted. It's not uncommon for our children to become the glue sticking the marriage together. What happens when the children move out, and we are left staring at our husbands, wondering if we even know the man we married? Our kids take up so much of our time and attention that some couples may turn a blind eye to the need to protect and grow their marriage.

Here are a few strategies to help strengthen your marriage, avoiding the prospect of a gray divorce:

1. Work hard *now* to communicate openly and honestly with each other. Be transparent. Tell each other how you feel and what you might be worried or concerned about in your relationship.
2. Make marriage a top priority.
3. Schedule date nights ... you'll find my list in the next chapter.
4. Do things you love to do together.
5. Pray together.
6. Get counseling if you feel you need it. Does your church offer marriage counseling? Take advantage of it. Or do you know an older couple with a strong marriage? Ask them for advice.
7. Don't be afraid to talk about money. You might each have your own thoughts and opinions on how your finances should be used. If you disagree on spending and investing, it can create much friction. Talk about a budget, how to plan for the future, retirement plans, etc. Discuss your concerns or disagreements about money

with respect for each other's opinions, heading off future problems.

8. How can you better share the responsibilities of running your household? Granted, now that the children are gone, there are fewer activities and chores to deal with. But you still need to come to an agreement about daily tasks and financial decisions. Try to share responsibilities as equally as possible.

9. Intimacy. This is critical for a healthy marriage. Physical and emotional intimacy. Take time together, have meaningful conversations with each other, listen, listen, listen.

10. Do you both share the same values and goals? It will draw you closer together if you can align your priorities and visions for your future.

11. Take care of yourself. See chapter 14 for tips.

With all the clamor and commotion kids bring into our homes, it isn't difficult to stop hearing each other. But when we listen to our husbands, responding thoughtfully and intentionally, we can get to the root of any fear, frustration, or concern they may be dealing with. Of course, listening respectfully to one another is always important, but even more so if we listen and make every effort to *hear.* As we do, we may find any conflict begins to fade.

♾

Susan

I've read and listened to many speak about how you need to cultivate a relationship with your husband throughout the parenting years so that you won't be living with a stranger when you are an empty nester. My husband works from home and is around all the time. So, we are not exactly strangers, but we don't have a whole lot in common.

I do plan on investing more in my community and volunteering with more organizations. But I also want to learn how to be okay with less activity and work on my marriage relationship.

❧

How can you begin to strengthen your relationship now? Encourage him. Tell him the wonderful qualities you see in him, the qualities that drew you to him in the first place and point out the positive. Schedule an actual getaway, even if it's only overnight. Watch funny movies and laugh together. Obviously, pray together. It can only draw you closer.

The empty nest is a gift to your marriage, offering a chance to grow closer, dream bigger, and love more deeply than ever before. – Kate

Discussion Questions:

1. How would you describe your relationship with your husband now that your children have moved out?
2. If you have made your children your main priority, what steps can you take to change that and press into your relationship with your husband?
3. Which of the strategies above can you begin to explore now, in your empty nest season?

4. What are some ways you can listen more thoughtfully and responsively to your husband?

Scriptures:

- *So do not fear, for I am with you; do not be dismayed, for I am your God. I will strengthen you and help you; I will uphold you with my righteous right hand.* Isaiah 41:10 (NIV)
- *Though one may be overpowered by another, two can withstand him. And a threefold cord is not quickly broken.* Ecclesiastes 4:12
- *Scarcely had I passed them when I found him whom my soul loves. I held him, and would not let him go.* Song of Solomon 3:4 (ESV)
- *I therefore, a prisoner for the Lord, urge you to walk in a manner worthy of the calling to which you have been called, with all humility and gentleness, with patience, bearing with one another in love, eager to maintain the unity of the Spirit in the bond of peace.* Ephesians 4:1-3 (ESV)
- *Therefore, as God's chosen people, holy and dearly loved, clothe yourselves with compassion, kindness, humility, gentleness and patience.* Colossians 3:12 (NIV)

Prayer for My Marriage

Lord, my season has changed in many ways, but I don't want my marriage to change in any negative way. Give me ears to hear my husband and to always respond in love and with kindness.

Now that the children are gone, he and I have to figure out what our relationship looks like as we will spend much more time alone with each other.

Help me make my marriage my top priority and show me the ways I can serve and honor my husband. Give us wisdom about financial decisions and how best to run our household.

I always want to be an encouragement to him. Show us where we need to make changes and give each of us the humility to make them. Let intimacy continue to be an important part of our marriage, drawing us together more deeply than before.

In Jesus' name,
Amen

CHAPTER 16

REDISCOVERING
DATING ... YOUR HUSBAND

Swallow moms are most likely already doing this. Robin moms have the desire to focus on their marriage relationship but need some encouragement. And most Mourning Dove moms will have to make a determined effort, allowing their marriage to become their new focus now that the kids are gone.

If going out is not in the budget, consider the fun activities you can do at home that don't cost much if anything. Here is a list of several different date night ideas to spark your imagination:

- Create your favorite homemade pizza together.
- Sign up for a cooking class and explore a new skill like baking bread or learning a new cuisine like Thai, Greek, or Indian.
- If daytime is more convenient and works better for your schedules, take a hike or ride bikes together. Live near the ocean? Soak up the sun and splash in the waves.
- Indulge in a spa night at home or book a couple's massage or spa treatment.

- Game nights can be a lot of fun, especially if you are competitive. Classic board games like chess or backgammon, card games, or video games are all good choices. Or tackle a new game together like *I Should Have Known That*, a fun trivia game, *The Hygge Game - Cozy Conversation in Pleasant Company*, or *Hyve*, a chess-like game featuring bugs!
- Plan a day trip to a museum or gallery you have always wanted to visit but could never find the time.
- Attend a live concert or show. Or be brave and go to karaoke … that is guaranteed to bring lots of fun and laughter! Spend your evening enjoying each other and making fun memories.
- Volunteer together at a homeless shelter, food bank, or animal shelter.
- Stay in and cook a romantic dinner. Try something you both love and choose a challenging recipe you have always wanted to tackle.
- Have a Stay-at-Home Date Night Picnic. Spread a blanket on the floor, make a yummy picnic basket, watch a movie and cuddle, put on some romantic music, light a few candles, put down your phones, and simply enjoy spending time together.
- Enjoy an online or video Bible study.
- Relax as you take a scenic drive. Enjoy the sights and the chance to have some alone time. Pack a lunch or some fun snacks for the ride.
- Tackle a home improvement DIY or craft project.

- Begin an online class to learn a new skill together or watch an interesting documentary about a subject that interests you both.
- Have a dance party. Put on some music and show off your amazing moves!
- Recreate your first date. Where did you go, what did you eat, and what was the most lasting impression of your husband?

The Lord has a plan for your marriage beyond children and parenting. Take time now to pray and assess what He may be calling you to as a couple.

Dads Have an Empty Nest, Too

You aren't the only one experiencing an empty nest. Dad may or may not have had the same degree or consistency of daily interaction with your children, but he, too, feels the loss and must learn to grapple and cope with his feelings. He might work from home like my husband did most of the time, or he works full or part-time out of the house. Maybe you do, too. But regardless, you will each experience the empty nest in your own separate ways.

Dad might not show his emotional side as easily as you do, but this season takes its own unique toll on him. Like you, he may experience sadness, loneliness, and a sense of loss. He must also learn to navigate a shift in his role and relationship with his children.

If he worked out of the house, he might not have had the same amount of time with the children that you did each day. But if he is like most dads, the time he spent with the kids doing all the dad things left an indelible mark on his heart.

> *God made men decidedly different, and your*
> *husband senses the loss in his own way.* – Kate

❦

Pamela

What we are learning in this empty nest season is sweet acceptance. We bicker less and offer so much more grace than we ever did before. We've laid down our need to be right. We desire cooperation over competition. We both win.

We no longer try to change one another, and we can appreciate how the other is wired. He's a detailed thinker, and I paint a broad brushstroke. Both of our perspectives are needed, and we complement each other perfectly. They don't cancel each other out.

Perhaps this season is the sweetest because we are not distracted by raising kids. We have time to study one another and appreciate our differences instead of being annoyed by them. We simply marvel at the gift of our relationship and God's perfect design for us.

❦

Dad may miss the time spent with his son or daughter going to sporting events or the man-to-man alone time teaching his boy the *man* things of this world. He may also miss special moments with his daughter, maybe regretting not having the time to spend with her that he would have liked.

Many men will suffer in silence, fearing that admitting pain might make them look weak or overly sensitive. He may recognize and regret that he bought into the lie that he needs to *man up* and keep his pain and feelings to himself.

Dads can descend into despair if they have trouble understanding or acknowledging what they are feeling and why they are feeling it. Be patient as your husband walks through this season with you. For insight into how fatherhood is changing, check out the MSN article in the resources listed at the back of the book.

Most fathers are deeply connected to their children and express the loss far more than dads did a generation ago. Dads of this generation spend more time and are more involved than ever in their children's daily lives. They will almost certainly express their sense of loss differently than you, yet they miss them just as much.

∽⌒

Roberta

I left my daughter at college and my husband left our son at his. They asked the parents to leave once they got through the formalities of instruction/directions. My husband got in his car and drove a bit before he pulled over to call me. He had a lump in his throat and was struggling to hold back tears, which is when it hit both of us.

I had said my goodbyes at home before they left, so I didn't have the same experience as my husband when he had to leave him at school and drive home by himself. It was much harder for him to physically leave our son than he was prepared for.

⤳

With their newfound freedom, dads have more time to focus on their own interests or hobbies. He may have new career aspirations, and the empty nest season affords him the option to work on those. It's a significant transition for dads, bringing challenges but also opportunities to grow and find a renewed sense of purpose.

As you step into your new season, in addition to doing what God is calling you to do, help support your husband's calling. God may be daring him to a new adventure, too. Whatever God is asking you to do should never be at odds with where God has called your husband. If it is, pray diligently to discern if it's truly His call. Get counsel and make sure you are not working against God's will.

Our Father is not the author of confusion, and neither strife nor contention is in His plan for your marriage. As mentioned in chapter two, God is a God of perfect timing, and He has an ideal season for you both.

Discussion Questions:

1. When you first met, what attracted you to your husband?
2. Why do you think you fell in love with him?
3. What did you love to do together before the kids came along?
4. If you still have younger kids at home, do you have a group of friends or grandparents willing to swap babysitting duties? If not, can you set something up?

5. What date night ideas do you think are fun and doable?
6. What about your husband...how is he dealing with the empty nest, and how can you support him?
7. Are you and your husband aligned with what God is calling you to in this next season? If not, what steps can you take to find common ground?

Scriptures:

- *Husbands, love your wives, just as Christ also loved the church and gave Himself for her.* Ephesians 5:25
- *Wives, submit to your own husbands, as to the Lord. For the husband is head of the wife, as also Christ is head of the church; and He is the Savior of the body. Therefore just as the church is subject to Christ, so let the wives be to their own husbands in everything.* Ephesians 5:22-24
- *And the LORD God said, "It is not good that man should be alone; I will make him a helper comparable to him."* Genesis 2:18
- *And above all things have fervent love for one another, for "love will cover a multitude of sins."* 1 Peter 4:8
- *My dear brothers and sisters, take note of this: Everyone should be quick to listen, slow to speak and slow to become angry.* James 1:19 (NIV)

A Prayer for Affection

Father, I'm grateful for the gift of marriage and I thank You for giving me my husband and for our bond and the commitment we have to each other. Now that our season has changed, we need Your wise counsel to understand how to strengthen and prioritize our marriage in this brand-new chapter.

Marriage is a sacred covenant You created as a reflection of Your love for us. Help me refocus and give attention to my marriage, investing time and energy into nurturing and reinforcing our bond. I can get distracted by the busyness of life. I need insight on how I can begin to carve out time to spend with my husband and ways to love and appreciate him every day and not get distracted by the busyness of life.

Fill our hearts with a renewed affection for each other and the desire to cultivate patience. We want Your will for our marriage, and we trust You will sustain us in every circumstance, big or small. Teach us to cherish our time together, making the most of every opportunity to fortify our relationship. Help us pursue new interests, create new memories, and continue growing together as the years go by.

Guard my heart against complacency or indifference. Motivate us to attend to our marriage with diligence as we remain intentional with our actions and words. May the Holy Spirit lay the foundation for our relationship, guiding us in love and grace.

Let each of us be quick to forgive, bearing with one another and serving each other every day. Thank You for our marriage, Lord. May it be an example to our children and to everyone else who may be watching. Above all, may our marriage bring glory to Your name.

In Jesus' name,
Amen

CHAPTER 17

Single Moms and the Empty Nest

The empty nest is tough enough for married moms, but what about a single mom whose last child has left home? Her home now seems doubly empty.

For the single Swallow mom, the empty nest might be that long-awaited season to reignite the dreams she laid down to raise her children. She anticipates this new stage with all its adventures and possibilities.

Single Robin moms look forward to their newfound freedom but with some apprehension. She knows she must let go of the past and move into a new way of thinking, understanding that there is a new chapter to explore. With some trepidation, she plants her toes into the future before fully stepping in.

Single Mourning Dove moms have a harder time finding the positive in an empty nest. They may continue to grieve the past and resist moving into their second act. It can take her a bit more time to recover from the sudden silence and the impact of her children heading out the door.

Life has revolved around your kids for nearly two decades, often letting friends and a social life take a backseat to parenting. The sacrifices you've made are exponentially more than the married mom. You have had fewer opportunities to sleep in, take alone time, or develop friendships. The empty nest can catch you off guard. But if you let it, it can provide the first opportunity in years to dream about what comes next.

While many moms struggle with negative emotions when their After Party begins, the empty nest can impact single moms even more harshly. It is natural to rely on your children for emotional support. After all, they were your responsibility for eighteen years or more. But now they're gone, and you are alone.

Jo

Single parenting is extremely difficult on many levels. Now that I'm an empty nest mom, there's a new dynamic. I'm aware that what I'm feeling is because I've allowed myself to feed into my empty walls. Hours can be spent sitting and staring into the nothingness.

I pace in a vacant child's room and entertain thoughts about what I could have done to be more connected to my children now that they've sprouted wings. I count down the hours till it's a reasonable time to go to sleep so I can be done with the weight of nothingness.

No longer do I check my phone for that missed call that isn't there. Calls only grace my phone when my grown kids have a need that their friend or father can't meet. I've allowed the empty walls to rob my joy, fog my hope, and leave me feeling invisible. My empty walls have taken me from being a parent to just a vapor. But each day, I try to take my eyes off myself.

❧

Not all single moms find the transition to an empty nest straightforward or simple to navigate. Are you irrelevant now that the kids are gone? No ... not by any means. Though every new season takes some getting used to, this upside-down feeling won't last forever despite how it feels.

You might have a job to occupy your time and attention, but without a husband, your nest can feel even emptier than a married mom's. You face a quiet and vacant home, and lacking a vibrant social life, this new world can seem overwhelming. But you have an After Party like any other mom! Dreams and adventures wait for you, too. Adventures you've always wanted to explore but never had the time.

Single moms, *you have permission to feel all the feelings without guilt.* Whether single or married, we will all grapple with a roller coaster of emotions as we shift from a vibrant home to an empty nest.

> *Celebrate your accomplishments as a single mom. This brand-new chapter is a beautiful testament to your stamina and strength.* – Kate

This is your opportunity to pick up where you left off before you had children. What were your personal passions back then? What did you set aside when you were parenting that you can begin to explore again?

Seek out groups and clubs you might want to join to meet other moms. While your children are still home, connecting with friends occasionally for coffee or lunch can help keep the relationships fresh. This new season is a great time to reignite friendships you may have set aside when your kids were home.

Join with other empty nesters, especially other single moms who have been through the transition. Their perspective and experience will help you see that this new season *is* survivable.

Most cities and towns have meetups for parents with grown children. If family is available, lean on them for support, or spend time with a sibling, reminding them that your schedule is less busy now and you would love the chance to get together.

Say yes when you get an invite to a social gathering, even if you have no desire to go. It might feel daunting at first, and you might not know anyone, but staying connected and reaching out can sidestep depression and self-pity.

Give yourself something to look forward to... a movie, lunch with a friend, an upcoming trip, or any other enjoyable activity that comes to mind.

Now that you have extra time, do something you love, something life-giving. Take a cooking or craft class, go bowling, work out at the gym with a friend, travel to those places you have longed to visit, go back to school, volunteer, or start that ministry or business you've always dreamt of. Depending on your job, any of these are available to you now. Embrace your independence and celebrate your accomplishments.

Stay in touch with your children. Maintain open communication and be the safe place they can land.

Build your social network. Join a group in your area, maybe something geared specifically toward single moms. Find a community that blesses and encourages

THE AFTER PARTY OF THE EMPTY NEST

you and consider reconnecting with the women's group in your church.

You are only limited by your desires and budget. You can now explore any and every opportunity you can imagine.

Call me crazy, but this might be a great time to consider dating. When our kids live at home, they can be convenient shields to bar us from facing the dating world. I understand it's an uneasy prospect if you have been single for some time. But meeting a man for lunch or coffee could be a safe on-ramp to possibly finding a deep and lasting relationship. Ask friends if they know someone who might be a good prospect. Many churches have fellowship groups for single or divorced adults.

There is more than one way to deal with the empty nest so it doesn't feel quite so empty. You have shouldered the burden and responsibilities of parenting alone, possibly for years. But help is available allowing you to get a handle on this new season.

Make an extra effort to care for yourself physically, mentally, emotionally, and spiritually. Find the time and the discipline to exercise and eat well. Do what you enjoy, and don't be afraid to ask for support from your friends and family. Most importantly, whenever you have extra time on your hands, spend it with the Lord and seek His wisdom about your future.

As you pray and sit in God's presence, He will show you that you are *more than a parent*. He will share His dreams with you and begin to reveal your next chapter and where He wants to take you. You may already know where that is. Now is the time to press in and get His direction for your next step.

Discussion Questions:

1. What joys are you hoping for in this new season? What sorrows are you experiencing?
2. What activities can you do now that you couldn't do when your children were at home?
3. What can you add to your thankfulness list?
4. How can you better take care of yourself in this new season?

Scriptures:

- *And my God will supply every need of yours according to his riches in glory in Christ Jesus.* Philippians 4:19 (ESV)
- *Behold, I will do a new thing. Now it shall spring forth. Shall you not know it? I will even make a road in the wilderness and rivers in the desert.* Isaiah 43:19
- *By faith Abraham obeyed when he was called to go out to the place which he would receive as an inheritance. And he went out, not knowing where he was going.* Hebrews 11:8
- *O LORD, You are the portion of my inheritance and my cup; You maintain my lot. The lines have fallen to me in pleasant places; Yes, I have a good inheritance.* Psalm 16:5-6

A Prayer for Wisdom for the Single Empty Nest Mom

Father, I've been alone for a while, but now, I feel more alone than ever. My house is too quiet and too empty, and I don't know exactly what I'm supposed to do. I need Your guidance to get me through this season and into the next one.

Teach me how to cope with these feelings of the loss and loneliness since my children left home. I am seeking Your strength to fully release them into Your care, knowing You have plans for their future, just as You do for mine. Continue to watch over them, guide them, and cover them with Your precious love.

What's next, Lord? I want to discern Your purpose for my life. Show me which opportunities to embrace and which to leave behind.

Remind me to maintain a grateful heart for all You've given me and the blessings surrounding me, even in the midst of change. Guide my steps, Lord. Help me build a life of purpose, joy, and humility. I know my only strength is in You. Draw me closer in prayer and Your word. I believe in Your provision to meet all my needs.

I give You my fear and anxiety, Father. I know You alone hold my future, and I trust you with it. Please shower me with Your peace that passes all understanding. As I walk forward with fear and caution, remind me that You are with me every step I take.

In Jesus' name,
Amen

CHAPTER 18

DEAR EMPTY NEST MOM: SELF-CARE IS NOT SELFISH

We know we should eat right … right? Get enough sleep, drink enough water, and avoid sugar, preservatives, white flour, and junk food. Let's examine some additional aspects of self-care.

Self-care has always sounded a bit *selfish* and unproductive, as if it's *all about me*, lavish and exclusive. Well, in a way it is, and there is nothing wrong with that. We are worth the effort. Why? Because the word of God tells us we are *"fearfully and wonderfully made"* in Psalm 139:14. If we neglect our health, we risk burnout, anxiety, depression, or worse. Our relationships with our family and friends can suffer.

> *If we are not pouring into ourselves, how can we pour out to others?* – Kate

Use every bit of willpower to avoid giving in to the lure to self-medicate in any number of not-so-healthy ways as you manage the start of your empty nest. We can rationalize the desire to overindulge in sugar-loaded foods or alcohol to help lessen the pain. After all, it's a major transition, upending our physical and emotional equilibrium, and the enemy's lie of false comfort is powerful. But that lie can be his evil ambush in disguise.

If we're not mindful, we risk creating a ticking time bomb in our future, including weight gain, despair, addiction, lost relationships, and other casualties.

The empty nest season is an ideal time to examine our choices and reordered priorities for genuine and God-honoring self-care. It's an opportunity to take a look at what's working well in our lives, honestly considering what needs to change.

❧

Monica

As an empty nest mom, I've learned the importance of self-care. After years of dedicating myself to raising my children, I found myself with an empty home and a need to rediscover who I am. I started prioritizing my health, taking time to exercise, eat well, and rest. I pursued hobbies I'd set aside and deepened my spiritual life. By investing in myself, I became stronger and more fulfilled. Self-care has allowed me to embrace this new season with joy and peace, proving that caring for myself is just as important as caring for others.

❧

Conduct a clutter cleanse! There are many categories of clutter: emotional, relational, and physical. *Declutter unhealthy relationships in your life...* those who don't support, uplift, or reinforce positive values and behaviors. They might need to go.

Evaluate your relationships. Revisit them to ensure there aren't people or their issues bringing negative vibes into your life. I have found, as many of us have, that not all relationships are meant to last a lifetime. People will come and go. We can learn to distance ourselves from those who drain instead of enriching our lives.

No one is required to maintain an unhealthy friendship, and it really is okay to move on. More than once, I've put wrong expectations on certain relationships, finally concluding that the relationship was based on their convenience, not on an intimate connection with me.

How can you gently detach yourself from the negative people in your life? Ask the Lord to give you the discernment to recognize those who feed you, drawing you higher, and those who stifle your well-being and your walk with the Lord. Some friendships are for a season, some for life. Take time to evaluate them and prayerfully determine if they are lifting you up or tearing you down. If you find you are not growing in Christ, and no one is encouraging you to go deeper, you may want to examine who you spend your time with. God will show you if you ask.

Invest time with people, especially other women, who model Christ in their lives. It will inspire you to dig deeper in your walk with the Lord. We will experience much growth if we're intentional about who we spend time with. If a relationship isn't encouraging us, we are allowed to wish someone well, say goodbye, and move on.

Author Jim Rohn taught that *we become the average of the five people we spend the most time with.* It is worth considering your five.

Declutter your home. Give away, sell, or throw away the items you don't need or want anymore. I have some lovely items, but why keep them if they are sitting in a cabinet gathering dust? It's gratifying to give away or sell unwanted clutter, and it feels wonderful to lighten your load. It can take a lot of stress off your shoulders and put a little extra money in your pocket.

We have a community garage sale once or twice each year which goes a long way to helping me minimize clutter. Donate what you are no longer using to a local ministry. Clean the cabinet under your sink, linen closet, and fridge. I love finally removing what's been hiding on the back shelf and regaining a sparkling clean, well-organized fridge!

As best you can, focus on the positive. We must be proactive in fighting depression and living in the past. They can lead to regret, anxiety, or worse if we don't continually fight them. It always amazes me how much it helps my attitude when I shift my focus to a positive outlook.

In this overly hyperventilating world, how do we find rest? Why do we need it?

Rest has purpose, and rest is productive. It's a precious gift to the ones who know how to use it.

Rest allows our bodies to rejuvenate, enhances our emotional well-being, and recharges us emotionally.

Rest allows us to pursue and strengthen relationships, cultivating greater intimacy. It's the kind of self-care that provides a healthy work-life balance and helps prevent burnout.

Rest stimulates creativity, giving us more energy and mental clarity.

And most importantly, rest provides all of us the opportunity to connect with the Lord. We have more time and mental space to engage in prayer and worship.

Here are twelve suggestions to encourage your self-care:

1. Head outside for some fresh air. Sometimes, the smallest changes can have the greatest impact on our health. Breathing in fresh air and taking time in the sun is a great way to take a break during the day. I am intentional about getting some sun every day if I have the time, even if it's a cloudy day. You can still synthesize vitamin D on cloudy days because full spectrum sunlight continues to occur behind overcast skies during any season. Ultraviolet (UV) light is required to produce vitamin D, which is present even on cloudy days. Full spectrum sunlight can even reflect off of buildings, sidewalks, and snow which can increase our exposure to UV rays. The sun provides essential vitamin D that can be difficult to get from our food alone, especially during winter.

2. If it's warm outside, take a cup of coffee, lunch, or your laptop and head outside for a sunny break. My husband and I are blessed to have a comfortable front porch, and on a warm sunny day, you can often find me out there reading, writing, and soaking up the sun.

3. Breathe deeply. Deep breathing, sometimes called diaphragmatic breathing, allows more air to flow into your body. It is known to calm

nerves, reducing stress and anxiety. As a trained singer, deep breathing was a consistent element emphasized by every one of my vocal coaches. Additionally, it can help improve your attention span and lower pain levels.

4. Open your home and reconnect with family and friends.

5. Surround yourself with positive people. They can bring joy and warmth, lending an ear when you are down or dealing with a difficult issue.

6. Climb out of your safe space. The After Party is a great time to dive into fresh experiences you always wanted to try but never had the time, finances, bandwidth, or courage to consider. Sign up for something that will provide a sense of accomplishment. Do it with a friend if you need that extra push

7. Establish community. Join a club or a class. Go to the women's meeting or Bible study at your church. Take a fitness class or join a life group. Start one if there isn't one.

8. Commit to eating as healthy a diet as you can. Real nutrient-dense food, not loaded with chemicals, seed oils, or preservatives, will nourish our bodies far better than fast food or processed junk food. We will feel better, look better, be less prone to illness, and have an easier time maintaining a healthy weight and life. Not to mention save money. Shop the outer edges of the grocery store where the real, fresh food usually lives.

9. Create peaceful surroundings. As mundane as this may sound, doing something simple like making your bed each day can genuinely help

you feel better. When I take time to straighten up the kitchen before I go to sleep, I can wake up to clean counters with no dirty dishes in the sink. Open a window or two to let fresh air in. Put on soothing music to take the edge off the day. Light a fragrant candle. Take a relaxing bath with Epsom salts or a scented bath bomb with your favorite essential oils.

10. Change your self-talk. Was I really a good mom? Did I mess up my child? Will they be all right on their own? Do I still have a purpose? Will my child want to spend time with me anymore? So many questions can hammer our hearts, making us feel helpless. We can change those negative statements into positive ones by turning them on their heads. Some examples: *"I did all I could to raise my child with love and care." "God has a brand-new chapter for me now that my children are grown and gone." "I have worth and value as a child of God, and He has a unique and valuable plan and purpose for me."*

11. Indulge yourself a bit. Now that you have more time, enjoy what you found harder to do when your children were home. Take a hot bubble bath while listening to your favorite podcast. Get a mani-pedi and talk to the girl tending to your feet and toes. Get those highlights in your hair you've always wanted. Indulge in a massage or a facial.

12. Count your blessings every day. If we're not careful, we can fall into a pit of self-pity in the wink of an eye. The best way to combat it is to maintain a heart of gratitude, thanking God for all the

amazing experiences and blessings He gives us. Take some time to make a gratitude list. Write out ten things you are thankful for today.

*Give thanks in everything. What's the
"everything" He's allowing right now?* – Kate

Pursue your purpose, not a career or job. Live each day with passion and gratitude. Don't just go through the motions every day, structure and discipline your time. Be present in the moment.

*Don't lament what you can't change or
worry about what's ahead. Know God has
you in the palm of His hands.* – Kate

In Hebrews 12:1, Paul encourages *let us lay aside every weight… and let us run with endurance the race that is set before us.* We need to run our individual races. Let's not quit at the starting line. Let's persevere and press in when we reach the messy middle of our After Party. Unleash your gift and finish strong!

We can thank the Lord for trusting us with the profound responsibility of raising the children He gave us. Thank Him for what you are going through right now, knowing in time, you will have the opportunity to encourage other moms entering their own empty nest season.

We all have much to be thankful for. 2 Corinthians 1:4 reminds us that Jesus *comforts us in all afflictions, so that we may be able to comfort those who are in any affliction with the comfort with which we ourselves are comforted by God.*

Discussion Questions:

1. What ten things you are grateful for in this season?
2. Are there people who introduce negativity into your life? How should you handle them?
3. What steps can you take today to begin decluttering your life, emotionally and physically?
4. What types of self-care can you begin incorporating into your life now that you are an empty nester?

Scriptures:

- *Or do you not know that your body is the temple of the Holy Spirit who is in you, whom you have from God, and you are not your own? For you were bought at a price; therefore glorify God in your body and in your spirit, which are God's.* 1 Corinthians 6:19-20
- *Forget the former things; do not dwell on the past. See, I am doing a new thing! Now it springs up; do you not perceive it? I am making a way in the wilderness and streams in the wasteland.* Isaiah 43:18-19 (NIV)
- *… who comforts us in all our tribulation, that we may be able to comfort those who are in any trouble, with the comfort with which we ourselves are comforted by God.* 2 Corinthians 1:4
- *Beloved, I pray that you may prosper in all things and be in health, just as your soul prospers.* 3 John 1:2
- *A cheerful heart is a good medicine, but a downcast spirit dries up the bones.* Proverbs 17:22 (RSV)
- *And do not get drunk with wine, for that is debauchery, but be filled with the Spirit.* Ephesians 5:18 (ESV)

A Prayer for Wise Choices

Father, I need Your guidance and help to make good, practical, and healthy decisions with my life and time right now. I know it's important to take care of myself as I have cared for others. But I seek Your wisdom for ways to create consistent boundaries for my life in all areas, including relationships and times of rest, rejuvenation, and relaxation.

I want to make choices that honor You, Lord. Your word tells us that our bodies are the temple of the Holy Spirit. Continually remind me of that scripture, especially when I'm tempted to overindulge. I want exercise, eating healthy, and getting enough sleep to become priorities. My body is a gift from You, and I need to treat it with honor and respect.

Please help me with my emotions as well. It's hard right now, and I've been tempted to move in unhealthy directions in some areas. Your strength alone causes me to stand firm against all temptation.

Remind me to make time for activities that bring me joy and fulfillment.

Above all, encourage me to make my relationship with You a priority in these hectic times. I need rest and renewal, and I know I can only find them when I spend time in Your presence. Let Your word be a source of delight.

Thank you for Your constant care and faithfulness. Your grace will help me make wise decisions so that I may continue to serve You and others with joy and love.

In Jesus' name,
Amen

CHAPTER 19

CHAPTER 15

HOW EMPTY NEST MOMS CAN BRIDGE THE GENERATION GAP: MENTORING MATTERS

An enormous gaping hole exists in the American Church—a giant generation gap between Baby Boomers, Millennials, Generation X, Gen Z, and beyond. The empty nest is a perfect season to pray about who God is calling you to mentor.

Why do we need to bridge the generation gap? God tells us to. This scripture from Titus 2 is not merely a nice thought. It's a stern command:

The older women likewise, that they be reverent in behavior, not slanderers, not given to much wine, teachers of good things—that they admonish the young women to love their to love their children, to be discreet, chaste, homemakers, good, obedient to their own husbands, that the word of God may not be blasphemed (Titus 2:3-5 NKJV).

I talk with so many disoriented and desperate young women who long for a mentor to help guide them through this morass of modern life. Too often, when approached by a younger woman asking for a mentor, we older women are quick to say no. Technology and social media have moved so fast that many of us are not as up-to-speed and technologically capable as the younger generation, which is intimidating, to say the least. Because we may not be as fully immersed in the current cultural mainstream as they are, many of us mistakenly believe the lie that we have nothing to offer, that we are irrelevant.

Women in my generation (Baby Boomers) have dropped the mentoring ball for the most part, and I am not sure why. Either they are so happy with their comfortable lives that they don't want to bother, or they mistakenly believe they don't have time or have nothing valuable to give a younger mom.

Some young moms have a pessimistic impression that the older generation is irrelevant. They are convinced we can't understand what they face in today's lunatic culture and, therefore, can't begin to help them. So, they turn to their peers for advice.

Many deal with insecurity as the trap of social media ensnares them in a web of unrealistic comparison and competition, leading to self-judgment and condemnation. Not to mention anxiety and depression. They may erroneously believe the lie that older women would never be able to understand the stresses of their lives. It becomes an easy excuse to avoid spending time with us.

Because we are from different generations, we truly can't understand all the confusing issues younger women deal with every day. Regardless, Scripture clearly instructs us to teach the younger. We have wisdom borne of the life experience young women need.

We can remain isolated from each other, but together, we can help one another navigate our world's chaotic and confused challenges to live full and rich lives ... lives that will mutually bless each other and knock out fear and intimidation.

When we've marinated in the empty nest for a while, and the tricky and complicated part of that transition is over, all three of our maturing bird moms will begin to recognize what type of younger bird mom she's choosing to mentor. Like often attracts like. In this case, that can be a good thing. She will recognize life's unhealthy pitfalls and give good counsel.

Mentoring passes on wisdom for personal growth for generations to come. We receive as much benefit and wisdom from the women we mentor as they ever get from us. They help keep us apprised of all that is happening in our culture, current trends we might have missed, and movements we may not be aware of. They help *us* as we encourage *them* in holiness and godly living.

As we live and explore the life God has called us to, we motivate and teach other women how to do the same. Our experiences, successes, and failures are invaluable to pass on to younger moms.

Younger moms need older moms to guide them through the treacherous minefield of life in the twenty-first century. None of us should have to do it alone. When we take the time to press in and encourage a younger woman, we bless her and reap positive benefits. As we make time to spend with young moms, they will present us with a refreshing take on culture, helping us better understand what they face each day, experiences we may not fully grasp because of context.

Benita

As an older mom, I've journeyed through the challenges and joys of raising children. Now, with my nest empty, I feel called to mentor younger moms. Sharing my experiences and lessons learned has been incredibly fulfilling.

I love providing a listening ear, offering advice, and watching these young moms grow in their confidence and abilities. Mentoring is a way for me to give back and to help create a supportive community where every mom can thrive. It's a blessing to be part of their journey and see our connection's positive impact!

We can counsel and advise a younger mom struggling with her marriage as she battles to raise her children in a world far different from the one she grew up in. We can support a single mom as she navigates her career and dating. As we listen closely to their needs and goals, we begin to build a strong bond founded on trust. As we share our experiences, both good and bad, and the lessons we've learned, we can offer sound advice based on our own successes and failures.

Most importantly, our circumstances are different from theirs. They face challenges far more daunting than we faced when we were raising children. We live in dangerous times, upheaval and chaos hides around every corner, deeply embedded in each branch of social media. What can we do? We can share our core values and time-tested beliefs. Ones that ground and stabilize us no matter what generation we belong to. The Bible has the only truth that won't waffle with all the cultural confusion surrounding us.

Mentoring encourages growth, both theirs and ours. Sometimes, a younger mom needs emotional or practical support in areas like discipline, marriage, or running the household. Being available and offering support can make all the difference, as it did for me.

When I was a young mom and a baby Christian, properly understanding biblical discipline stressed me out. I did not know what was biblically sound and what was not. I felt at a complete loss and sought wisdom from a group of older women who were further along in their mothering journeys. They helped me uncover scripture-based best practices for disciplining consistently and wisely.

It helped tremendously. After receiving wise counsel and guidance, I took their advice. From that moment, the atmosphere in my home converted from chaos to peace. I knew I had much to learn in many areas, and their wise guidance proved invaluable.

***

Jillian

As a young mom, navigating motherhood often felt completely overwhelming and isolating. I realized I needed lots of guidance and support, so I sought out a mentor. Having an experienced mom to turn to has been a game-changer.

My mentor provides practical advice, shares her own experiences, successes, and failures, and offers encouragement when I need it most. Her godly counsel, wisdom and understanding have given me confidence and peace of mind.

Mentoring has shown me that I'm not alone and that I can thrive as a mom with the right support.

❦

Don't hesitate to offer honest feedback in a kind, respectful way. Help a younger mom identify areas that need improvement, gently steering her away from an unbiblical path she may be heading down and compliment her in the areas where she is excelling. Your grace and maturity will provide the insight and discernment she might be desperate to find.

Let her see you embody and model the qualities and behavior you hope to see grow in her. Demonstrate what godly marriage, biblical child-rearing, housekeeping skills, and living with integrity look like.

The young woman you mentor isn't looking for perfection from you. She is looking for women whose marriages, lives, and parenting styles she can emulate. She's looking for *you.* When you feel drawn to a particular young woman, invite her to lunch. Get to know her with no agenda, and you may find you have made a great friend and possibly have started a mutually beneficial learning experience.

Don't wait for her to come to you. Be willing to open your home and your heart. Mentoring requires time and effort and the willingness to invest in another's growth and development. It does not have to be formal, it can be as simple as going out for coffee once a month, inviting her over for lunch, starting a crafting project, or gardening together. Or it can be as formal as a weekly Bible study and anywhere in between. Offer hospitality.

If you are a younger mom, are there older women in your life mentoring you and pouring their years of wisdom into you? Or are you out there on your own, navigating life's turbulent waters as best you can but desperate for help from someone who has been there and done that?

What about you older women? Do you feel disconnected and irrelevant to the younger women you know? Are you intimidated by technology and social media? Do you feel just plain uncool and out of touch? Are you afraid to commit the time to discover the blessing in connecting with the generations younger than you?

The Mentorship Model

The tender and beautiful story of Ruth and Naomi in the Bible beautifully illustrates a strong cross-generational relationship. Ruth, a Moabite and a Gentile, observed her mother-in-law Naomi, and noted her persistent faith as Naomi resolutely trusted God, even amid tragedy and loss.

Ruth proved her deep devotion and unabashed loyalty by following Naomi into a culture and country utterly foreign to her. Despite adversity, her heart was deeply drawn to something she saw in Naomi that she could neither name nor live without, a devout worship of God amid hardship and heartbreak. Despite Naomi's misery and her resignation to an unknown future, Ruth risked it all to follow her. Ruth's loyalty and faithfulness to Naomi placed her squarely in the lineage of Christ.

God took two very different women, one a Jew and one a Moabite, one old and one young, and knit them together in a beautiful mutual mentoring relationship. We can glean much from Ruth and Naomi as we witness how Naomi invested in a younger woman. I encourage you to read the short (four chapters) but powerful book of Ruth.

You cannot find the word "mentor" in the Bible, but the concept runs throughout. Moses' father-in-law, Jethro, mentored Moses. Moses mentored Joshua. Elizabeth mentored Mary, Mordecai mentored Esther, and Naomi mentored Ruth.

So, what exactly does it take to be a Titus 2 Woman? She is a woman who behaves with reverence. She uses her words to guide, teach, and heal. She is marked by moderation in all things, and her appetites are disciplined. She walks her talk and is willing to train younger women in how to live a life pleasing to God. She loves, serves, and respects her husband, and loves her children.

Many younger women, regardless of whether they know the Lord or not, battle with stress and self-focus from the never-ending deception of constant comparison. This leads to insecurity and judging themselves harshly for failing to attain some misty ideal of a life they're convinced they must obtain. How many of us believe we don't measure up to the carefully curated lives we see online? How easily we are deceived about both our identity and purpose.

It starts with us. We see the problem, and we can do something about it. If you are younger, find an older woman whose life exudes the fragrance of Christ. If you are older, seek out a younger woman and make a point to pour into her life with humility and grace, helping her submit her life to the Lordship of Jesus Christ.

Be honest with your own struggles and let her see that you are far from perfect. Ask questions and listen more than you talk. Give advice sparingly. Offer her the practical help she needs. Reassure her with your words, write an encouraging note, invite her to coffee, and commit to praying for her.

Younger women, respect her age and the life lessons she's learned. Listen and ask questions. Find a woman strong in her faith, living with integrity, who has raised her children well, and who trusts God in tough times. Ask her to pray with you, as she may be uncomfortable pushing herself forward.

None of us have all the answers. But when we humble ourselves and <u>INVEST</u> in another, we will be amazed how much richer life becomes.

This acronym describes the ideal mentoring relationship:

I – Instruct
N – Nurture
V – Venerate
E – Encourage
S – Stay
T – Treasure

Is God showing you someone right now? The women He puts in your life deserve your sacrifice, service, and commitment. Will you wash their feet, love them, challenge them, teach them, learn from them, listen to them, laugh and cry with them? Can you imagine what would change in the church and in the world if we pledged to be in a relationship with the women around us? Let's commit to being Titus 2 women together!

Ask God if one of the purposes He has for you in your empty nest season is to serve as a mentor for women yet to experience an empty nest. We need each other. Older women need younger women, and younger women need older women. As the world grows darker by the minute, we can stand side by side.

We are a far more powerful force against the enemy together than we will ever be apart. – Kate

Be willing to say yes when she asks, and do not fear becoming a Titus 2 woman. You have much to share. True, godly, and honorable women should desire to develop a heart to teach and mentor the younger generation. Titus 2 women are sorely missing in the church, but the world urgently needs them pouring into the next generation.

Galatians 3:28 tells us, *There is neither Jew nor Greek, there is neither slave nor free, there is neither male nor female; for you are all one in Christ Jesus.*

I think it would be fair to consider that there is neither young nor old. It's about sharing the love of God and the new life we find in Jesus Christ.

Ladies, we need each other! I need you younger women, and you need me and others my age. I need the life wisdom of women even older than me.

Young moms may understand how to navigate the internet and all its shortcuts. But let me assure you, one generation *does not* have it all.

There are substantial differences between us, but how we respond to them is key. We see multiple generations in the church, each worshipping the same God, yet I see the gap widening, causing a disconnect and a general drifting apart. The Bible says we serve the God of Abraham, Isaac, and Jacob, three generations right there!

Division is not God's best for any of us. Our common enemy seeks desperately to divide, but God desires unity among the generations.

The empty nest years may be the perfect time for what you thought you'd set aside to now be poured out into a younger generation who needs a mom figure or a godly mom mentor.

Discussion Questions:

1. Are you mentoring a younger mom? If so, what are you learning as you spend time with her?
2. If you're a younger mom, are you willing to be mentored by an older woman?
3. If you aren't mentoring now, what is hindering you?
4. Is God showing you someone right now that you can mentor or be mentored by?
5. Are you willing to ask a younger woman out for coffee or lunch, etc. to get to know her? If not, why not?
6. What are some ways you can invest in and nurture a younger mom?

Scriptures:

- *... the older women likewise, that they be reverent in behavior, not slanderers, not given to much wine, teachers of good things—that they admonish the young women to love their children, to be discreet, chaste,* *homemakers, good, obedient to their own husbands, that the word of God may not be blasphemed.* Titus 2:3-5

- *As iron sharpens iron, so a man sharpens the countenance of his friend.* Proverbs 27:17
- *One generation shall praise Your works to another, and shall declare Your mighty acts.* Psalm 145:4
- *Give instruction to a wise man, and he will be still wiser. Teach a just man, and he will increase in learning.* Proverbs 9:9
- *Likewise you younger people, submit yourselves to your elders. Yes, all of you be submissive to one another, and be clothed with humility, for "God resists the proud, but gives grace to the humble."* 1 Peter 5:5

A Prayer for Mentoring Wisdom

Lord, my heart is to mentor other women, especially moms. It's more critical than ever and I am well aware how much the generations need each other. If a younger woman asks me to mentor her, move me to say yes and be a willing vessel to make the commitment to spend time with her.

Each generation has much to learn from the other, none of us have it all.

As I've walked with You through the years, You've given me insight into the needs of younger women and my own need for wise counsel. I pray I can provide that to another woman sharing and modeling the principles found in Titus 2.

Create in me a true and loving heart to pour out what You have poured into me. Help me provide that wise counsel to a younger woman.

Let my life and all I've learned be a beacon to the women You bring to me. I want to lead them to You and *Your* truth, never mine. I pray my life will reflect the goodness and compassion You have shown me all these years, continuously pointing them back to You.

I pray for the courage to step out and embrace each opportunity You bring me. Use me to be a role model and make a difference in their journey and relationship with You.

I thank You for the ability to mentor other women and I pray You will show me women who can mentor me.

In Jesus' name,
Amen

THE FUTURE

CHAPTER 20

HINDRANCES TO YOUR AFTER PARTY: SIX TRAPS THAT COULD FRUSTRATE YOUR FUTURE

The enemy of our souls is determined to derail our dreams, our purpose, and our impact when our after-party kicks in. Hindrances and outright obstacles may hit us straight on, and it is our choice to tolerate them or fight them. What are some hindrances scheming to get in the way of your future?

1. *Fear.* It can be daunting to walk into the future God has assigned to us. There is a price to pay when we step into any new role or path Jesus is revealing to us. It takes living a life of faith to walk where God calls us. We can find a way to gather the courage to fight the lies swirling in our heads. Our lack of faith denies God's power and character, calling God a liar, and not trusting that He will do what He says He will do. Is it scary to take on a new thing? Yes. It will be scary.

Sometimes, we have to *do it afraid*. But when we give into fear, we can forfeit our destiny.

If we based our usefulness and purpose on our history and past sins, none of us would qualify. I am grateful each and every day that God sees me according to my *destiny*, not my *history*.

2. *Unbelief.* Before meeting the Lord, I had no interest in getting to know Jesus or accepting Him as Savior. After an abortion at eighteen and leaving home, I spent *years* pursuing fame and fortune in the Broadway theatre world. I met my husband while starring in the Broadway National Tour of The King and I, opposite Yul Brynner. When we met, Mike was the associate conductor, and we fell in love across the footlights. We married and continued to focus on and invest our time and effort in our careers.

We never pursued God, but despite not understanding our need for Him, *He* pursued *us*. After ignoring God for years, we ultimately recognized the true state of our lives without Him. At the height of our careers, we invited Jesus into our hearts and committed to follow Him. Jesus had every right to judge us. But He did not. Why? Because His love forgave and covered our sins. Because we've been justified by our faith in Him and have repented. Because we gave our hearts, souls, and lives to Him, Jesus wiped away every sin we ever committed…and nailed them to the cross.

3. *Self-doubt and negative self-talk.* Who has the right to tell any of us we're not smart enough, or too old, or don't have what it takes? Who has our

permission to say that we are not good enough and will *never accomplish anything?* Do we believe *them,* or do we believe *God?* The enemy loves to pursue and hound us, quietly whispering that we should cling to a pessimistic view of ourselves, scattering fault lines through our minds and poisoning our thoughts. Satan's goal? Prevent us from seeing ourselves as God sees us.

God reminds us that we are … *accepted in the beloved* (Ephesians 1:6). His word declares that we are blessed, bold, beautiful, adored, cherished, chosen, and so much more. How many of us believe He can't use us? We convince ourselves that God does not even see us or that we missed our moment. Or one of the biggest lies of all, "I messed up too much, why would He ever use *me?*

4. *The land of good enough.* Why do we continue to bombard Him with our feeble reasons to excuse ourselves from His divine nudge? We forget He chose us before the foundation of the world *with* a purpose and *for* a purpose. Satan's goal? To confuse us so we do not recognize who we are or *Whose* we are. And when we don't know who we are, the devil can talk us right out of our destiny.

It is easier than we think to settle for what I like to call "the land of good enough." Far too many of us don't live up to our potential. It is so much easier to stay comfortable, floating aimlessly through life, not willing to step into God's future.

Are we content to sit home or to trust the Lord and pursue excellence in the area God has called us to? Excellence honors God and the trust He has placed in us by giving us specific gifts and callings. Excellence is simply going beyond what is expected, rising above the world's standard, and leaving the world better than we found it. We strive to be the best we possibly can with the gifts and talents He has given us, with humility, understanding we aren't in competition with others.

Complacency is the enemy of purpose. – Kate

It isn't hard to live without faith or hope for our future. We have the right to choose to live unexceptional lives, undemanding and comfortable, boring, and bereft of purpose. How many of us will sacrifice the good to attain the best? We all need a perspective shift, realizing God created us for divine reasons. *We are here on purpose.*

5. *Negative opinions from relatives and friends.* No one can shoot down our dreams faster than family. They see us in a very specific way, and if we upset their idea of who we are, they will try their hardest to fit us back into the familiar box they've kept us in for decades. They are comfortable with who they believe us to be, and when we change, they don't know what to do with us. We can *never* be who God called us to be if our family continues to remind us of who we are not.

Family and friends may try to convince us *that we are not who we were.* They're exactly right! Because of what God has done in us, we are not who we were *anymore.* Even Jesus's family did not respect or believe Him at first. Don't let the dream thieves steal your future.

6. *The trap of offense.* This hateful hindrance will suck you in if you let it, making you believe you have every right to be offended and angry. What they did was so unforgivable! And it probably was. But we have no right to hold onto offense or unforgiveness ... ever. Not for an hour. We must let it go. We need only look at how much the Lord has forgiven us and how much sin Christ took on our behalf!

If you can be offended, you will be offended. – Kate

Do the opposite of what the enemy is trying to convince you to do. When he tries to sell you on the satisfaction of holding onto offense, let it go and forgive, and instead, serve the ones who mistreated you. The Beatitudes teach us to *do good to those who hate you, and pray for those who spitefully use you and persecute you* (Matthew 5:44). I learned this the hard way. There is no other way to learn how to *pray for those who spitefully use you* until you have been spitefully used.

This phrase struck me years ago, and it's how I visualize forgiveness. *Kiss the stones that bloodied your feet.* It is one of the hardest things we will ever do but it will transform our relationship with the One who gave His life for us.

Let this scripture help you rethink holding onto offense and unforgiveness: *For if you forgive men their trespasses, your heavenly Father will also forgive you. But if you do not forgive men their trespasses, neither will your Father forgive your trespasses.* Matthew 6:14-15

When we are offended, we have two choices. If the offender is harmful and detrimental to our lives, we do not have to spend time with them. We have every right to walk away from the relationship as we continue to pray for them.

We must do whatever we have to do to forgive and let go of any offense we face today. It is not easy, and admittedly, I still struggle with it at times. But it is a necessary step if we are going to grow in our relationship with the Lord and walk into the future He prepared for us. Let us become women who *cannot be offended*, women quick to forgive no matter what. Let us wear humility as a garment, *even as offenses try to flatten us.*

Humility before honor, forgiveness
before favor. – Kate

Let's discover a new depth to all of that in these important empty nest years.

God has numberless ways to test our obedience, and offense is one of them. Let us determine not to get caught in its trap, because if you *can* be offended, you *will* be offended.

Discussion Questions:

1. What is the biggest hindrance standing in the way of your After Party?
2. What lies are you telling yourself that might prevent you from walking into the new adventure God has prepared for you?
3. Are you becoming complacent? Why?

4. How can you change that?
5. Is your family affecting your future? How?
6. Who do you need to forgive?

Scriptures:

- *A man's heart plans his way, but the LORD directs his steps.* Proverbs 16:9
- *For even His brothers did not believe in Him.* John 7:5
- *He came to His own, and His own did not receive Him.* John 1:11
- *... that you do not become sluggish, but imitate those who through faith and patience inherit the promises.* Hebrews 6:12
- *He who has a slack hand becomes poor, but the hand of the diligent makes rich.* Proverbs 10:4
- *The way of the lazy man is like a hedge of thorns, But the way of the upright is a highway.* Proverbs 15:19

A Prayer for Humility

Father, my heart is weighed down by the challenges and uncertainties I'm facing right now. You know my struggles. Struggles with fear, self-doubt, unbelief, offense, and more. All can overwhelm me if I dwell on them. But I choose to lift my eyes to You because You alone are the author and perfecter of my faith, I know I can't do it by myself. And I know You are bigger than any challenge or problem I may encounter that seeks to hinder me and push me off my path.

I ask You to help me release all feelings of bitterness and offense against every person who has hurt me or misunderstood me. Remind me to walk in love even when faced with criticism and lies. Fill me with Your peace, Lord.

Show me how to cast off every spirit of fear that seeks to paralyze me and prevent me from walking in my gifting. Help me remember all Your great and precious promises to me and make me fearless, unafraid to trust You, even when I can't see how to move forward.

I pray You will always remind me of who I am in You whenever doubts and insecurities rear their ugly heads. Remind me that I am Your beloved child, chosen and redeemed by Your grace. When I start to slip into negative self-talk, silence that voice and replace it with Your truth, knowing I am fearfully and wonderfully made in Your image. Guard my heart against all skepticism, unbelief, and negative self-talk. Help me walk in faith, believing that Your promises are yes and amen.

Lord, I am eternally grateful for Your presence and provision amid every challenge the enemy throws at me. I pray Your peace will continually guard my heart and my mind, and may it set me free from every chain that seeks to bind me and push me off the path of righteousness.

In Jesus' name,
Amen

CHAPTER 21

IF YOU DON'T KNOW WHERE YOU'RE GOING, HOW WILL YOU KNOW WHEN YOU GET THERE?

Understanding and exercising the power of goal setting are two of the most valuable gifts we can give ourselves. Your nest may be empty, but now is the time to begin making and setting out to achieve new goals for yourself. If we don't know where we are headed, how do we know when we get there?

It's important to focus on the results we are looking for to avoid wasting energy and wandering aimlessly through this season. When we know where we are headed, we can discern when we've arrived at our goal. I find great comfort in clarifying a current goal. It motivates me to keep pressing forward. The clearer the goal, the more apt we will be to stick with pursuing it.

We have always been a S.M.A.R.T. goal setting family and have seen its power over and over in multiple areas of our lives—personal, financial, spiritual, and physical. This method of writing down specific, measurable goals was first developed by George T. Doran, a Canadian business consultant in the early 80's. His methods have helped many people and motivated them to work toward achieving them.

Statistics abound indicating that those who set written goals are drawn like magnets to reach them. There are so many great resources available on goal setting, but this basic outline is a good one to get you started if this is new for you, or if you're wondering how to apply it in your empty nest years.

- State your goal as a positive statement. *I will finish my college degree in nursing.*
- Be precise and specific. *I will finish my college degree in nursing by the spring of next year.* Use dates, times, and amounts so you can measure your results.
- Prioritize your goals and revisit them regularly.
- Commit your goals to writing and put them in a place where you can see them daily. Some like to make a vision board or dot the mirror or computer with goal-affirming notes as a visual reminder.
- Specify and write down the steps necessary to achieve your goals.
- Set deadlines and attach intermediate timelines to your goals. Go back to school? Take an online course? Find a mentor?
- Consider the obstacles to achieving your goals and develop a plan to deal with them.

This simple acronym is a handy way of reminding us that our goals should be SMART: **S**pecific – **M**easurable – **A**ttainable – **R**elevant – **T**ime-sensitive

Look for others who have accomplished their goals in your field or area of interest. Get to know them and discover how they have done it. There is always more than one path forward, and by talking with others you will be inspired to find yours.

Discussion Questions:

1. Have you sat down and begun to set goals for your future yet?
2. What is your biggest fear in the goal-setting process?
3. Are you writing your goals down? If not, how can you begin?
4. What results are you looking for?
5. What positive statements can you use to begin setting goals for your future?
6. How can you partner with God to set goals?

Scriptures:

- *May he give you the desire of your heart and make all your plans succeed.* Psalm 20:4 (NIV)
- *Delight yourself also in the LORD, and He shall give you the desires of your heart.* Psalm 37:4
- *Without counsel, plans go awry, but in the multitude of counselors they are established.* Proverbs 15:22
- *Commit your works to the LORD, and your thoughts will be established.* Proverbs 16:3
- *For which of you, intending to build a tower, does not sit down first and count the cost, whether he has enough to finish it.* Luke 14:28

KATE BATTISTELLI

A Prayer for Perseverance

Father, I'm in a brand-new phase of life and I know You have a plan and a purpose specifically for me. I need your help to understand and recognize the power of setting goals and how important it is to embrace them as a tool to shape and define my future.

Give me the wisdom to set only the goals that are aligned with Your will for my life and the courage to diligently see them through.

Show me the perfect direction to take so I don't waste my time pursuing goals that aren't from You. I want my life to glorify Your name, but I need help figuring out my next step. I need clarity of vision, wisdom, and discernment to know what is from You and what isn't.

Help me set specific, measurable, attainable, relevant, and time-sensitive goals. Let them align with Your kingdom purposes, bringing honor to Your name and representing You well.

Give me the strength I need to overcome any obstacles or challenges I may face. I pray for perseverance no matter what setbacks may come, and I trust that You will see me through.

Help me guard my mind against all comparison and competition, reminding me to run the race You have given me, not to try and run another's, knowing You have a unique calling for *me* to fulfill.

Thank You, Father, for the reminder that the ultimate purpose of goals is to ensure that I will know when I get where You have ordained me to go. I pray the Holy Spirit will guide every step I take.

In Jesus' Name,

Amen

CHAPTER 22

CATCH AND RELEASE

It's a push/pull, this mothering business. Holding on while at the same time, letting go.

As our tiny, helpless, beautiful babies arrive, we vow to hold them close, keep them safe, and never let the world and all its fears, worries, and heartaches get too close. We become mama-fierce, protective as she-lions, ready to devour any who try to harm them.

And all along, we applaud each move toward independence. *"She lifted her head!" "He rolled over!" "She sat up!" "Look at him walking—such a big boy!"* They grow as each day, each year, we teach them how to do it on their own.

We remind her, *"You're a big girl now."* We cheer him on when he climbs a tree. And we hug and hold them close the first time we let them ride the school bus, wiping away our mama-tears. And we *let* them ride. We let them grow.

The seasons and years spin faster and faster, and we keep letting go. Letting them learn and then letting them do it alone. Letting them make mistakes. Letting them fall and letting them fail. Our hearts want to protect and shield, but if we hold too tight, we will stunt their growth and hold them back. The truth we must face is this: every day, our children need us a little bit less.

We cry and worry and pray as we realize that *parenting is only a part of our journey, it's not our whole life.*

Our children create their own lives, and they will be drawn to a variety of new and different interests. Remember when they used to like everything you liked? They wanted to be *just like you.* But now, off they go. They have changed and so have their tastes.

They are interested in things that you never in a million years imagined. And that's okay. But admittedly, it is weird and takes some getting used to. *"She used to think this was so cool." "He used to love doing this." "Who is this kid?"*

If we are doing it right, we raise to release. We love to let them go. We let them be who they were created to be.

We send them out into the world and marvel and applaud as they find their way and discover their own lives. We are the foundation. They start here but grow to become so much more as our ceiling becomes their floor.

The best time to begin preparing for the After Party is *now*… because if we are doing it right, we are raising them to let them go. We are raising them to leave the nest, training them to live on their own, and cheering them on from the sidelines when they go. And that's the hardest part.

Because they *do* go. Because mothering is a journey of letting go … a holy release made possible only by holding onto the One that matters most.

Like little slippery fish, we catch them, hold them for a moment as the sun glints on their strange, silvery skin, and then we throw them back. If we hold on too long, they'll gasp for air, suffocate, and stink up the boat. Fish were not created to breathe our air; they must breathe their own in the setting created and perfectly suited for them.

God gives us our beautiful little fish, these shimmering, silver-skinned lives to hold and mold for a season. Then He expects us to give them back, to catch and release, to let Him do with their lives what He will.

It is by far the toughest part of parenting, this holy, hard giving back... this sacred release into God's mysterious purpose. We are *fishers of men* in more ways than one.

And we cling to the One who called us. We thank Him for the gift of raising our beautiful slippery fish as our hands and hearts prepare to let them go into all the world, the deep ocean of His purpose.

And we breathe, and we pray. *And we release...*

CHAPTER 23

LET'S PARTY!

Trust me mama...the After Party is good. You earned it, and you definitely do *not* want to miss it!

Raising a child who is comfortable enough to spread their wings means you've done your job well. Our role? Enable them to leave the nest, break free from limitations, and fly solo. – Kate

When you were a new mom with young children, you could barely wrap your brain around the thought of them *ever* leaving home. As they grew, you found parenting embodied the dichotomy of both holding close and letting go.

The most amazing thing I have noticed about my After Party? It has gotten progressively better and more rewarding with each passing year. No matter if you're a Swallow Mom, Robin Mom, or Mourning Dove Mom, your After Party is nothing to dread. Instead, it's an exciting and captivating season you can anticipate and relish. The After Party is something you *can* and *want* to prepare for.

When that day arrives, you'll discover that life is more than carpooling, laundry, and cries of "Where are my shoes?" You now have the opportunity to act on the dreams you deferred to deal with the awesome responsibilities of raising your children. If you still have littles at home, be patient and enjoy the season you're in. It may feel like it will never change. *It will.* God will dare many of us to do more than we ever believed possible during this empty nest season. But here is my last question–will you trust Jesus with your future?

Our empty nests *will* arrive, whether we want them to or not. In nature, mama birds often coax their babies out of the nest with a little push. Just as your children must fly into their futures, so must you. I'm giving you that little push and my prayer is that you will spread your wings and venture out into God's purpose for the second half of your life.

There *is* a second act, a future with your name on it, different from your children's but filled with hope and surprises you cannot begin to imagine … *if* you plan for it, believe in it, and, with the Lord's help, walk fearlessly into it. Why?

Because mom is not your only name.

Your invitation to the After Party awaits.

A Prayer for the Mom Who Has Launched Her Last Child

Lord, as my last one leaves the nest, I pray You will be with my child as they move out into the world and that You will be with me as I begin a new season.

It has been many years since I have been home alone and I pray You will remind me that my active time of mothering with children at home was a finite season, but not my only season.

Father, I know You have plans for me far beyond what I can see, plans to use me for Your glory, and I'm confident You will lead me and direct my steps in this new season of solitude.

Help me recognize Your voice when You speak and give me the courage to step into the next adventure You have designed for me.

Help my child begin to live out the lessons I diligently taught and to remember those lessons when the world, the flesh, and the devil try to draw them away from You and into sin. May Your voice in their ear be louder than the world's.

Be with them wherever they go and deliver them from evil.

Thank You for the divine opportunity to be a mom and to raise and train the children You gave me to love and serve You.

As this unfamiliar season looms, remind me that You have an entirely *new* season in store for me, and my future lies safely in the palm of Your hand.

In Jesus' name,
Amen

FOR ADDITIONAL READING

Chapter 1
The Empty Nest Syndrome, PsychCentral.com
https://psychcentral.com/health/empty-nest-syndrome#empty-nest-defined/

Chapter 5
Statistics on Raising Only Children
https://amyandrose.com/blogs/parenting/only-child-statistics
Empty Nest and Menopause
https://grownandflown.com/menopause-empty-nest-syndrome-answer-yes/

Chapter 6
Ruth Bell Graham's Poem for Prodigals.
https://billygraham.org/story/ruth-bell-grahams-5-truths-on-prodigals-and-those-who-love-them/

Chapter 12
Millennial Dads
https://www.msn.com/en-us/lifestyle/lifestyle-buzz/millennial-dads-shatter-stereotypes-triple-

time-spent-with-kids-compared-to-previous-
generations/ar-AA1n9Dsb
Empty Nest Dads
https://www.nytimes.com/2014/09/21/opinion/
sunday/sad-dads-in-the-empty-nest.html

Chapter 14
**The Effect of Diaphragmatic Breathing on
Attention: Negative Affect and Stress in Healthy
Adults**
https://www.ncbi.nlm.nih.gov/pmc/articles/
PMC5455070/

Chapter 17
Goal Setting
https://hqhire.com/goal-setting-statistics/

ACKNOWLEDGMENTS

No one writes a book alone. The right people walk beside us, helping us press through until we write the final word.

The journey of creating *The After Party of the Empty Nest* has been a shared one, and this book is a testament to the incredible support of those mentioned below. Their guidance made this dream a reality, and for that, I am deeply grateful.

To my husband, Mike. You have always loved, supported, encouraged, and believed in me, especially when I didn't believe in myself. Thank you for reading every word and giving me ideas and suggestions that make me a better writer. You have stuck with me these many years, and I am deeply grateful you walked with me into my own empty nest with grace and persistent encouragement, constantly reminding me that God's second act for me was right around the corner. Your support gave me the courage I needed to dive fearlessly into my own After Party.

To Francesca Goodwin. Being your mom has been the joy of my life. My nest may have emptied when you walked into your future, but watching you become a wife, mother, and passionate woman of God has filled my heart.

To Cynthia Ruchti, literary agent extraordinaire. Without your tireless and generous love and support, I could never have finished this book. You are so much more than an agent. You provided what I needed exactly when I needed it, and I'm beyond grateful for your wisdom, counsel, encouragement, and much appreciated and thoughtful critique of my work. This book is due to your unwavering belief in me and your gentle yet firm direction when I got off course. I am beyond blessed to have you on my side, and I look forward to many more projects together.

To Susan Salley, I sincerely appreciate your insightful editing skills. Your keen eye quickly picked up what I missed, and your suggestions significantly improved my manuscript.

To Hannah Linder, thank you for your beautiful book cover. You interpreted my ideas perfectly, artfully bringing them to life.

To Jill Kemerer and the talented team at Story Architect. This book wouldn't be possible without your guidance and support. Thank you for all your help with every single detail. I am confident this is the first of many endeavors together.

To the brave moms who generously contributed their stories to *The After Party of the Empty Nest*, your courage to share your raw and transparent stories—the good, the bad, and the broken—will inspire and give hope to the many women experiencing the significant sea change of the empty nest. Every one of your stories resonated with me, and I'm confident they will bless the moms reading this book. Your words will help guide many moms as they navigate this unsettling season, transitioning from an empty nest to their After Party. It's an honor to partner with you.

Thank You, Lord, for daring me to pick up my pen and write when I had no desire to become a writer. I took Your dare and because of Your love, patience, and guiding hand, I have discovered a beautiful mission field I never expected.

Lord, you are my God;
I will exalt you and praise your name,
for in perfect faithfulness
you have done wonderful things,
things planned long ago. Isaiah 25:1 NIV

About the Author

Kate Battistelli is the author of the bestseller, *The God Dare: Will You Choose to Believe the Impossible* and *Growing Great Kids: Partner with God to Cultivate His Purpose in Your Child's Life.* She's a contributing writer to Jordan Rubin's *Maker's Diet Meals, The (In)courage Bible for Women* and *The Spirt-Led Woman's Bible.* Her writing has appeared in *Guideposts, The Joyful Life magazine, The Better Mom, Mici magazine,* and more. Kate is one-third of the popular *Mom to Mom Podcast* and is an inaugural honoree with *She Leads Tennessee.*

As a young actress in New York City, Kate had a life-changing experience, going from understudy to starring as Anna in the Broadway National Tour of *The King and I* opposite Yul Brynner for more than 1,000 performances. Kate and her husband laid down their careers in the Broadway theatre in answer to their first "God Dare", moving out of New York City and into a life of homeschooling and home business.

She's been married to her husband Mike for more than four decades and loves living in Franklin, Tennessee near her daughter Francesca, son-in-law, and seven amazing grandchildren. Kate's heart is to serve women of all ages by mentoring and encouraging them to step out of their safe space and into His irresistible future.

OTHER BOOKS BY KATE

The God Dare: Will You Choose to Believe the Impossible?

Deep down inside, you know you're on this planet for a reason. God has a plan in mind just for you. In fact, He chose you for His plan before the foundation of the world. He created you precisely for this time and place, and He's perfectly equipped you to accomplish His purpose on the earth.

Through engaging and memorable true stories–both biblical and deeply personal–join Kate Battistelli as she challenges and encourages you to discover how God has specifically designed you for this time in history, your place in the world, and your role in His cosmic plan. Once and for all, let go of your fear, worry, pride, and strife...

All God ever needs is a willing vessel. Will you say yes to His dare?

Growing Great Kids: Partner with God to Cultivate His Purpose in Your Child's Life

Successful adults don't happen by accident. It takes wisdom to raise your children with a strong sense of their destiny in God and a deep knowledge of their gifts and callings.

In *Growing Great Kids*, Kate Battistelli shares what she and her husband, Mike, learned about parenting during the journey raising their daughter, GRAMMY® award winning artist, Francesca Battistelli. Using personal experiences to illustrate the insights she and her husband gleaned from God's word, she provides practical advice including:

- How to dream God's big dream for your child
- The value of humility and integrity
- How to interpret God's seasons in your child's life
- The power of a parent's words, and much more